CHOCOLATE

CHOCOLATE

90 Sinful and Sumptuous Indulgences

ELISABETH JOHANSSON

STERLING EPICURE

New York

"THE BEST CACAO BEANS MAKE THE BEST CHOCOLATE."

CONTENTS

FOREWORD

I have always loved working with chocolate, and writing this book has long been a dream. It feels extra fun to make this book right now, when chocolate is finding its way back to its roots. Cacao beans have long been overprocessed, which has resulted in a refined chocolate that is simultaneously impersonal and industrial. Now people are beginning to return to chocolate's origins in terms of cultivation and manufacturing. Organic and biodynamic farming has found success with good output and strong demand. Modern chocolate manufacturers are handling chocolate with greater delicacy, and it has once again become possible for small artisans to make good and sought-after quality chocolate. People have also begun making raw chocolate, which means that neither the cacao bean nor the chocolate has been heated over 108°F. Raw chocolate retains many of its natural and beneficial nutrients and has a softer and richer aroma than it does when the beans are roasted or when the chocolate is warmed to traditional temperatures. Raw chocolate that contains 99–100% cacao has a very soft and delicate flavor.

It's been 15 years since first I came in contact with high-quality chocolate. At that time, it was something fairly new in restaurant kitchens. A colleague showed me how to temper chocolate in a crème fraîche container—luckily, I was unaware of how complicated it is and how much training it requires in order to perfectly temper chocolate. We microwaved and stirred the chocolate feverishly for all the decorations that would be sent out with the desserts. A whole new world was unfolding.

Some years ago I made a chocolate guide for Paris and had the opportunity to meet the living legend Monsieur Poussin from Debauve & Gallais—Paris's oldest chocolate boutique, opened in 1761. That man, the seventh generation of chocolate makers, knew exactly what he was talking about. The chocolate he treated us to, the boutique's 99% chocolate and pralines, was absolutely among the best I have tasted! It was also exciting to meet Catherine Cluizel, daughter of the legendary Michel Cluizel, who makes wildly popular chocolate bars sold all over the world.

In this book you will get a lot of chocolate history but most of all a lot of useful information and a number of recipes. Follow me into my world of chocolate!

Elisabeth Johansson

THE CACAO TREE AND THE BEANS

The cacao tree or *Theobroma* (Greek for "food of the gods") originates from South and Central America. It grows geographically in a belt—the so-called cacao belt—that stretches around the globe across South and Central America, Asia and Africa, from 20° north to 20° south of the equator in tropical climates. It needs a temperature of at least 75°F and steady rainfall.

The trees grow to between 13 and 65 feet tall. The flowers are small, ¼–⅓ inch in diameter, and look like small orchids. They are white or light pink in color. The flowers grow in clusters directly on the trunk or on thicker branches. This growth method is called cauliflory. The fruits—or cacao beans—grow on older branches or directly on the trunk. They are cultivated in various ways just like wine grapes, depending on where they grow. Soil quality ("terroir"), climate, and different bean varieties give character and taste to chocolate in the same way grapes lend distinctive tastes to wine. Even a blend of cacao beans determines the taste of the final product, one that can be powerfully peppery, creamily toffee-like, or acerbic and mild, or have the taste of dried fruit, red berries, licorice, vanilla, or coffee.

Cacao beans are usually divided into three types: criollo, forastero and trinitario. In recent years, however, it has been shown that all three presumably originate from the same bean: criollo. For me, this was new information I experienced firsthand when I went to Ecuador, where brand-new American research was the topic for lively discussions about the DNA of cacao beans. It will be really exciting to follow developments in this area. One thing we already know is that different beans contain different amounts of pure criollo genes, and that in order to be classified as pure criollo, the fruit must contain at least 84% criollo genes.

CRIOLLO

Criollo (Spanish for "native") is the most exclusive cacao bean and earns the title "Grand Cru" for its high quality. It grows in, among other places, Mexico and the Caribbean; the West Indies; Madagascar; Java, Indonesia; and on islands in the Indian Ocean. The bean has a fine, delicate flavor and is a little acidic, but is difficult to grow, is sensitive to diseases and parasites, and delivers a small yield. The criollo family consists of several different beans: among others, the ocumare, porcelana, and chuao. The ocumare is a bean of very high quality that gets its name from the city Ocumare de la Costa. It is stout and rugged and has a coarse texture. The color can vary from almost white to pale violet. Porcelana is a much sought-after and exclusive bean that is cultivated in places such as Venezuela, Mexico, and the West Indies. The bean is light in color, sometimes almost white; when it ripens it becomes light green and eventually orange-red. The shell is thin and fairly soft. Chuao comes from a region in Venezuela also called Chuao. There used to be pure criollo in Chuao, but soon people began growing trinitario and forastero, and the varieties became intermixed. Still, the beans are of high quality.

FORASTERO

Forastero (Spanish for "foreign") is the most common cacao bean. It is easy to grow, gives a large yield, and has strong resistance to disease. It is slightly bitter and powerful in flavor. Forastero is grown in the Ivory Coast in Africa, Central America, South America, and the West Indies, along with New Guinea.

There are many different types of forastero, and the majority of them are used in blends. Amelonado was the most commonly grown forastero bean up until the 1950s. Cacao Nacional (Arriba) is a type of amelonado and is grown in Ecuador. It is a little sweeter and not as bitter as other amelonado beans. This bean is considered one of the world's finest, and has been called Fine Grande. Another type of forastero bean is para, which has a strong flavor and distinctive character.

TRINITARIO

The Spanish cultivated criollo on Trinidad during the 1600s. In 1727, the island was hit by a hurricane and a hybrid of criollo and forastero arose. When the hurricane passed, the plantation was destroyed and replanted with forastero. There appeared a spontaneous crossing between the new forastero and criollo that had survived the storm.

The cacao bean trinitario has inherited its taste from criollo and its hardiness from forastero. Trinitario beans that contain the greatest proportion of criollo are the most sought after. Today trinitario grows in South America, the West Indies, Sri Lanka, and Indonesia.

WILD CACAO

Wild cacao grows in South America in Bolivia, Venezuela, and Ecuador, as well as in other places. It was the agricultural engineer Volker Lehmann, a western European, who "discovered" the wild cacao bean in the Bolivian part of the Amazon during a trip with a local guide.

The wild cacao from Bolivia is especially distinctive due to its very high quality. For that reason, one of the world's foremost chocolate makers, Swiss chocolatier Felchlin, uses it. Beginning in 2005, Felchlin was the first to produce chocolate from wild cacao beans for commercial use. Their label is called Bolivia Cru Sauvage 68%. These small cacao beans have an extremely deep, rich, and nutty cacao flavor without any bitterness at all, which is unique.

In Sweden, Malmö Chocolate Factory, in cooperation with Danish chef and restaurateur Rasmus Bo Bojesen, has created the chocolate Oialla, made with wild cacao beans from Bolivia. Both the freshly roasted cacao beans and the ready-made chocolate have a well-balanced, soft, and pure flavor.

PROCESSING THE CACAO BEAN

QUALITY

There are different grades of beans. Varying amounts of cacao are used in chocolate, which is measured as a percentage of cacao content. Ultimately, what gives chocolate its flavor is the quality of the cacao bean, bean type, geographic region, and cacao content. It is common to blend different types of beans in order to get a good, original flavor. Roasting or drying (the beans used in raw chocolate are not roasted but are dried) also influences the final result. The chocolate's processing, rolling, and conching determine the consistency and taste.

FERMENTATION

There is a fermentation process used with cacao beans. A normal fermentation time for forastero and trinitario beans is about 5 days. For criollo beans it's a little faster, and they're ready in 2–3 days. Fermentation causes the beans to develop a chocolate flavor and removes some bitterness. In order to keep the fermentation consistent, beans are mixed during the process. This happens in specially built boxes constructed in "floors" with trapdoors through which the beans pour down in batches. At the place in Ecuador where we watched the fermentation, people used old paddles as a tool for stirring the beans. This is called box fermenting. Banana leaves were also used in the fermentation. Banana leaves contain a fungus (microbes) that helps expedite the fermentation, a common method used in organic manufacturing. There is also pit fermentation, which is common in Africa and involves digging pits and lining them with banana leaves.

DRYING

After fermentation, the beans are dried. The most traditional way to do this is to sun-dry the beans and move them several times a day. This is, however, work that requires both time and space. It is important to keep the beans free from moisture and rain, so large, thin, water-resistant blankets that let in sunlight are stretched across the beans. Industrial drying uses the aid of warm air pumps. The acetic acid built up during the fermentation is removed during the drying process, along with almost all the water, until only about 7% of the water content remains.

POLISHING

After drying, the beans are polished in large machines with rotating blades. Afterward, the beans are sorted and classified by size and quality, either by machine or by hand.

ROASTING

Roasting is a very important part of the manufacturing process. Temperature and roasting time produce different characteristics in different beans and determine aroma and flavor intensity. Temperature and time are adjusted depending on which type of bean will be roasted and the desired final result. Temperatures can range from 230 to 300°F. The beans are roasted for 20–50 minutes. After roasting, the moisture content in the beans is around 2½%. Raw chocolate is not roasted, only dried, which delivers a richer flavor profile.

BLENDING

For the chocolate maker, the bean blend is as important a choice as grapes are to the winemaker. This is the base on which the final product's taste and character are built.

CRUSHING

The crushing of the beans occurs in large machines where shell residue is finally trimmed or weeded out. The crushed beans are called nibs or grué.

ROLLING

Milling, or grinding of the beans, usually happens in batches on rollers. First they are ground to a dry mass that later converts to liquid form when the fat is released. The substance called cocoa liqueur, the cacao mass, is the base material in all chocolate production.

CONCHING

After the milling, different products are added to the base material. The fewer the products added, the higher the quality of the ready-made chocolate. Cacao butter, raw sugar, and conventional sugar are the most common. After that vanilla is added, which enhances the chocolate flavor. Powdered milk is added in milk chocolate. Emulsifiers are also common, such as soy lecithin or sunflower lecithin, which are added in order to improve homogeneity and hold. Exclusive chocolate uses only cacao butter as an emulsifier. Other vegetable fats are added as well. Here there are strict rules as to what and how much may be added in order to truly be called chocolate. Conching is a technique in which the mixture is processed in constant motion in large machines. Length and intensity vary greatly depending on the manufacturer, mechanical equipment, and the desired final result. In this phase the chocolate becomes shiny and refined. Moisture content sinks even further, the last traces of acetic acid disappear, and the chocolate becomes smooth and homogeneous. This technique—discovered and patented by Rodolphe Lindt—is the basis for all modern chocolate manufacturing.

RAW INGREDIENTS DERIVED FROM CACAO BEANS

cacao mass (opposite page, top)
cacao butter (opposite page, center)
cacao nibs (opposite page, right)
cacao powder (opposite page, bottom)

ADDED INGREDIENTS

These vary depending on what chocolate will be produced, but here are some of the most common:

raw sugar, sugar
vanilla, vanilla extract
soy lecithin
powdered milk (for light chocolate, milk chocolate, and white chocolate)

SOY LECITHIN

Vegetable oil made from soybeans. Used as an emulsifier in order to bind together different ingredients for a homogeneous consistency.

VANILLA

Used as flavoring. Vanilla extract is also used.

DARK CHOCOLATE

Contains cacao base, cacao butter, sugar, vanilla, and sometimes lecithin. The cacao content in dark chocolate usually ranges from 47 to 70%. It is most common to use a chocolate with 56–65% cacao when incorporating chocolate into cakes, cookies, ice cream, and mousses. When the cacao content exceeds 60%, the chocolate begins to have a powerful cacao flavor. There is even chocolate that contains 70–100% cacao content, but that is used most often as a flavor enhancer. The flavor can vary enormously and be slightly tart, fruity with vanilla notes, rich like caramel, and full bodied with taste of roasted, dark coffee, all depending on quality, geographic location, cultivation, bean variety, roasting, and blend.

MILK CHOCOLATE

Contains cacao base, cacao butter, sugar, powdered milk, lecithin and sometimes vanilla.

Cacao content in milk chocolate is usually 28–33%, but can, in better products, vary between 39 and 40%.

Milk chocolate has a mild cacao flavor with hints of caramel, nuts, and vanilla, and usually is a favorite of children. Just as with dark chocolate, there is a rise in popularity of milk chocolate with higher cacao content, which results in a kind of "medium chocolate," at 40–50% cacao.

WHITE CHOCOLATE

Contains cacao butter, sugar, powdered milk, and sometimes lecithin, along with sugar that is sometimes flavored with vanilla and is conched with pressure in order to obtain the best possible results. White chocolate is extremely sensitive to changes in temperature and requires care when melting or tempering.

TEMPERING

TEMPERING

Working with chocolate often requires a technique called tempering—a hardening process that makes chocolate stable so that it ultimately solidifies without splotches and gives it a nice shine. Tempering chocolate is a skill that requires practice in order to master it. It is also the most critical moment in the chocolate-making process that determines success when molding pralines, dipping candies, or making fine chocolate decorations.

The three factors that influence tempering are temperature of the chocolate, temperature in the room, and the time it takes to complete the process. The primary goal is to get the fats in the chocolate to solidify in the right way and make the chocolate homogeneous.

Perfectly tempered chocolate is shiny and fine on the surface without dull blemishes. It will also tighten slightly and shrink when it hardens—that is what makes it release from molds and praline forms. After that, the chocolate maintains its hardness at room temperature without splotching or losing its luster. If you have molded chocolate bars, for example, the chocolate will be so hard that it makes a snapping sound when you break it. It is difficult to temper small quantities of chocolate. The simplest way is microwave tempering in a microwave-safe glass or plastic bowl. If you melt chocolate in a microwave, it's best to microwave in short intervals, stirring frequently, especially with light chocolate (milk chocolate) and white chocolate, which contain the heat-sensitive milk protein casein. If you warm light or white chocolate too much, it will shrink and become hard, making it difficult to melt.

It also works well to melt chocolate over a water bath. Chop the chocolate and place it in a stainless steel bowl. Place the bowl on a pot with about 2 inches of boiling water. Make sure that the bowl covers the entire surface of the pot so that the chocolate isn't exposed to the steam, or place plastic wrap over the bowl. Let the chocolate melt.

Because white chocolate, milk chocolate, and dark chocolate are made up of different ingredients, they are tempered at different temperatures. It is important to maintain the chocolate's high quality. Different chocolate brands also temper in slightly different ways depending on the contents and the combination of ingredients. Here you can try different methods. Use a digital thermometer to measure the temperature. Good quality thermometers quickly show exact temperature changes, which is a big help when tempering chocolate. They are available at well-stocked cooking stores.

TEMPERING DARK CHOCOLATE

Finely chop the chocolate and melt two-thirds of it to **122–150°F**. Add the remaining chopped chocolate, and stir until the temperature lowers to **81–82°F**. Then gradually warm up the chocolate to a working temperature of **88–90°F**. The chocolate is now ready to use and will be shiny and break with a snap when it hardens.

TEMPERING MILK CHOCOLATE

Finely chop the chocolate and melt two-thirds of it to **113°F**. Add the remaining chopped chocolate, and stir until the temperature lowers to **79–81°F**. Then gradually warm up the chocolate to a working temperature of **86°F**. This takes only a few seconds in a microwave; the chocolate is now ready to use.

TEMPERING WHITE CHOCOLATE

Finely chop the chocolate and melt two-thirds of it to **104–113°F**. Add the remaining chocolate, and stir until the temperature lowers to **79–81°F**. Then warm up the chocolate to a working temperature of **84°F**. This takes only a few seconds in a microwave; the chocolate is now ready to use.

TEMPERING RAW CHOCOLATE (DARK CHOCOLATE 70–100%)

Warm this kind of chocolate to **113°F**. This gives it a smooth and solid tempering. The best temperature, of course, is **108°F**, which is as near the raw-food ideal as possible.

Finely chop the chocolate and melt three-fourths of it to **113°F**. Add the remaining chopped chocolate, and stir until the temperature falls to **81–82°F**. Then gradually warm up the chocolate to a working temperature of **88–90°F**. This takes only a few seconds in a microwave; the chocolate is now ready to use.

TABLING

Tabling is the tempering technique in which melted chocolate is chilled down over a cool surface, such as a stainless steel table, or a surface of marble or polished granite. This technique is usually used for a large quantity of chocolate.

Finely chop the chocolate and melt in a microwave oven or over a water bath to **131°F** for dark chocolate and **113°F** for light chocolate (milk chocolate) and white chocolate. Pour three-fourths of the melted chocolate on a marble or granite surface. Quickly spread out the chocolate with the help of a large putty knife or scraper (a painter's scraper with a plastic handle is easier to get clean than one with a wooden handle) and a large, thin metal icing spatula. Work the chocolate inward toward the middle with the help of the scraper and spatula. Remove the chocolate from the utensils by scraping them against one another so that the chocolate cools evenly to **81–82°F**.

Scrape the chocolate together and pour back in the bowl with the remaining melted chocolate. Blend together and gradually warm to **88–90°F** in the microwave, stirring it now and then. Now the chocolate is ready to work with. Maintain its temperature by warming the bowl and surface very briefly with a kitchen torch, or by microwaving it occasionally.

MICROWAVE TEMPERING EQUIPMENT

Digital thermometer
Glass or microwave-safe plastic bowl
Microwave oven
Rubber spatula or large plastic knife

TABLING EQUIPMENT

Digital thermometer
Glass bowl or stainless steel bowl
Stainless steel, marble, or polished granite surface
Carpenter's scraper or putty knife
Long thin metal icing spatula
Kitchen torch

DIPPING

Dipped items coated in tempered chocolate such as marzipan, truffles, or caramels need to maintain a temperature around **68°F** (room temperature), never in the refrigerator, which hardens the chocolate from the inside and turns it dull and gray. The best dipping temperature of tempered chocolate is **84–86°F**—if the chocolate is cooler than that, it can be too thick and make dipping difficult.

COOKED SUGAR BALL TEST

When you cook caramel, stir it now and then so that the caramel doesn't burn on the bottom. Avoid stirring it too much or the caramel may easily crystallize. Toward the end, when the sugar reaches about **239°F**, turn down the heat so that it doesn't burn. At **252°F**, cooled cooked sugar is still fairly soft, but at **255–257°F**, it starts to become sticky and hard. It can be difficult to measure the temperature when boiling sugar because the mixture is warmer at the bottom than on the surface. Therefore it's a good idea to do a ball test. Drop a little cooked sugar or caramel into a glass of ice water. If the sugar forms a fixed drop or a ball, then it's ready.

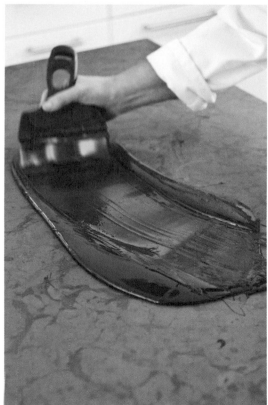

WORKING WITH CHOCOLATE

MOLDING PRALINE SHELLS AND CHOCOLATE BARS

Chop, melt, and temper the chocolate. Use a praline mold, preferably hard plastic. Feel free to try an old, metal vintage model found in antique stores. Clean the forms with a cotton ball or swab. If using an older model, you can polish them with a little melted cacao butter. Warm the forms just a bit with a kitchen torch and pour in the chocolate, filling each compartment. Tap the forms on a table several times so that all the air bubbles disappear. Let the form stand for 30–60 seconds and then turn upside down so that the excess chocolate runs out onto some parchment paper or the marble surface. If you are making chocolate bars, just scrape the excess chocolate off the form without inverting it. Use a scraper or a metal icing spatula to scrape off the form just before the chocolate has hardened. Let it solidify at cool room temperature or alternatively place the form in the fridge for 10–15 minutes. Once it solidifies completely, it will shrink and come loose from the forms.

Pipe the filling into the praline shells. If the filling is too liquid, let it harden before sealing the pralines. Seal the pralines (brush with tempered chocolate) and let the chocolate harden at cool room temperature for at least 6 hours. Remove the pralines by tapping the forms lightly upside down on the table. Do this carefully or else all the pralines will come loose at the same time. Chocolate pralines keep best at a temperature of **61–64°F.**

MOLDING CHOCOLATE SHARDS

Pour melted, tempered chocolate on a piece of heavy plastic or acetate. If you want to flavor the shards, sprinkle some crushed licorice, cacao nibs, or spices such as ground cinnamon or anise over the chocolate.

To make patterned chocolate shards use either a confectioner's embossing tool or a gum paste cutter. Draw patterns using white chocolate first and let it harden. Then cover with dark chocolate using an icing spatula and let it harden. You can also use plastic pattern sheets with various designs, such as crocodile skin and tree designs. There is even a special rubber scraper that gives chocolate shards a wood-like grain. Also, you can mold chocolate using transparent film, Bubble Wrap, and oil cloth with different textures. These materials are available at cake decorating and cooking stores.

ECUADOR– A COUNTRY IN THE CACAO BELT

JOURNEY TO ECUADOR

Gentle clouds hover over a beautiful landscape formed from black lava, volcanoes, and a dense, green forest. We are in Amazonas, home to some of the world's most varied species of flora and fauna. It is here that the cacao tree presumably originates. Researchers used to believe that the cacao tree had its origins in Mexico, but more likely it is in these ancient forests that it began growing some 4,000 years ago.

Ecuador in Amazonas is one of the countries that has been said to have the best cacao and chocolate in the world. After a long journey, photographer Susanna Blåvarg and I land in a Quito flooded with water (it hasn't rained that much in 15 years!), but thankfully we are met by our driver Jorge and our guide Willy. They will take us on a 5-hour trek into the interior, along the river Napo, past the city of Tena, straight into the jungle where we will spend the following days. During the trip, the sun comes out and the water disappears slowly from the flooded areas. I observe the landscape as it whizzes by. Here cacao beans grow in different districts and therefore taste totally different: beans that carry an earthy, mineral taste from the region of Manabí with its volcanic soil, and beans with a flowery character and hints of fruit and red berries from the region of Esmeraldas, where they grow oranges.

The ancient people of these regions have harvested cacao beans since before recorded time and have used them both for their own sake and as a livelihood. At one time different buyers came to visit and bought up the cacao beans, which left the people at a disadvantage as they were easily deceived into thinking that there were no real scales and fixed prices. Now there are cooperatives that set fair prices and help with selling the beans.

Having reached the area around the Napo River, we set off into the jungle early the next morning. After an hour's walk with our local guide in dense terrain, we catch our first glimpse

of a gigantic wild cacao tree, with beautiful purple-red cacao beans and the characteristic camouflaged tree trunk that glimmers green, silver, and gray. . . so beautiful and mighty! We stay as long as we can without the ants under our feet carrying us away. We wander a little farther to a fantastic waterfall where we bathe in crystal-clear water, then continue on through the branches and vines where there are even more wild cacao trees, both large and small, with red, green, and yellow cacao beans. A wonderful experience that exceeds all my expectations!

Now it's time to visit one of Karrari's cacao-growing native families. We travel by canoe down the Napo River for several kilometers, then climb back onto land in order to hike to our host family that consists of a mother, father, and eight children. It is common for Kichwa families to have many children; these are the farmers who live in the jungle. The curious children come running toward us, as visitors aren't a part of everyday life here. The Kichwa family invites us to share a native drink while they show us their medicine cabinet with medicinal herbs and plants that grow locally. Then it's time to step into the jungle vines and harvest some cacao beans. We savor the sweet, soft white contents of the cacao pods that are amazingly good and fresh, almost like a hard fruity caramel. The children love to suck on the beans within the white capsules that enclose the bean. There is, on the whole, plenty of food in the jungle. These small-scale growers run mixed-growth farms with cacao, bananas, papaya, chili peppers, corn, cassava, sugarcane, and whatever else they need.

We also visit a little native village where people grow, among other things, cacao and papaya. We buy schoolbooks and pens for the 24 children in the village, and are in turn invited to share their maito, fish grilled in banana leaves over an open fire. After the meal, the indigenous people invite us to dance with the women. Some of the men don't take part in this. After the dance, I will get to prepare cacao from the ground. What luck! I never imagined in my wildest dreams that I would get to stand in a hut in a native village and roast cacao beans over a fire! Now I stand here with all these children, dogs, young mothers, and older women at a hot pan filled with newly harvested cacao beans. The beans take time to roast, and I get a little sweaty constantly stirring the beans so they don't burn. One of the young women loans me a macramé bracelet with scarlet good-luck beads that one of the women has been making. They hand it to me together with my new name: "Hard-working mamma"!

When the beans are ready, they are poured quickly onto a banana leaf on a large table in the middle of the hut. Everyone, large and small, hurries over to help rub the skin off the beans by hand while they are still warm. They are ground several times and then are mixed together with raw sugar, cornmeal

RECIPE FROM THE ORIGINAL INHABITANTS

Here are some "native recipes," namely native cacao recipes, directly from the Ecuadorean jungle!

WARM CHOCOLATE WITH LEMONGRASS

The indigenous people add lemongrass to their warm chocolate, partly for flavor's sake, and partly because of lemongrass's antiseptic qualities, which are good for the stomach. You can also flavor this drink with cinnamon or vanilla.

2 LARGE CUPS

1 stalk of lemongrass
1¾ cups water
3 tbsp cacao powder
5 tsp raw sugar
1¾ cups milk

or powdered milk, and hot water boiled with lemongrass. Lemongrass is thought to be good for digestion and gives the cacao a fresh flavor. When the cacao is ready, the children run into the forest and pick sun-ripened papayas and banana leaves. The papaya is cut and sliced into small pieces, which are then spread over the banana leaves. Finally, the freshly roasted, creamy, and lukewarm chocolate is poured over the leaves. A little boy gets ahold of the empty chocolate bowl and licks the lovely leftovers. No doubt he forgets both time and space!

Split the lemongrass lengthwise and lightly crush the fibers with a mortar or the back of a knife. Place in a pot. Pour in the water and boil for a few minutes. Add the cacao and sugar and continue boiling for a few minutes. Strain. Simmer the milk and whisk it vigorously so that it becomes foamy. Pour the chocolate mixture into large cups and add the frothy milk.

TRUFFLES WITH ROASTED JUNGLE PEANUTS

Wherever the cacao tree grows, there are fine peanuts with a thin, striped shell on the inside that have a deep and concentrated peanut flavor.

ABOUT 30 PIECES

1¾ oz shelled jungle peanuts or regular peanuts
9 oz dark chocolate (64–70%)
Scant ½ cup heavy whipping cream
2 tbsp honey
½ cup (40 g) cacao powder, for rolling

Roast the peanuts in a dry frying pan. Chop the chocolate and place it in a bowl. Bring the cream and honey to a boil and pour the mixture over the chocolate. Stir until all the chocolate has melted. Fill a disposable piping bag with the truffle mixture and let harden. Pipe lines of the chocolate, about 1 inch wide, on a baking sheet lined with parchment paper. Slice into approximately 30 pieces. Press a few peanuts into the center of each piece and form into a ball. Sift cacao powder on a plate and roll the balls in the cacao.

CHOCOLATE ICE POPS WITH COCONUT AND CHOCOLATE SAUCE

Ice cream of the simplest variety is sold at the local market and in small cafés in the city of Tena.

4 PORTIONS

¼ cup cacao powder
Scant ½ cup raw sugar
⅔ cup water
4 wooden Popsicle sticks
¾ cup coconut cream
¾ cup coconut milk
Shredded coconut, for garnishing

Bring the cacao, raw sugar, and water to a boil in a saucepan; reduce the heat and let simmer until the sauce thickens. Drop a teaspoon of chocolate sauce in the bottom of four plastic cups and place a Popsicle stick in each one. Whisk the coconut cream, coconut milk, and ¼ cup of the chocolate sauce together. Divide the mixture evenly between the cups and freeze them overnight. Remove the cups and rinse them quickly in lukewarm water. Free the ice pops from the cups. If you want, you can dip the ice cream in the remaining chocolate sauce or in melted chocolate, and coat them in shredded coconut.

THE KALLARI COOPERATIVE

The Kallari Cooperative in Ecuador ("kallari" means "to begin") was started in 1997 by Diego Greffa and is today a successful cooperative that produces and sells one of the world's best quality chocolates. "Organic chocolate in harmony with nature" is its motto.

The thought behind the cooperative was to give the young indigenous Kichwa people and mestizo farmers the opportunity to diversify their farming and support themselves while doing it. The plants, which the farmers have the opportunity to buy at fair prices, are grown in simple greenhouses. The trees themselves can be harvested after 1½ years, and they are productive for about 20 years.

Today, 850 families are associated with the organization and 4,000 people work there. The families work together so that the fathers can be near their children. The cooperative's first step was selling coffee beans and cacao beans. During the past decade, the focus has been on chocolate manufacturing. Kallari had, and continues to have, the goal to produce the best quality chocolate, which is entirely possible given that Ecuador has some of the best beans in the world. To grow and manufacture the chocolate organically was a given from the start. Today, the children learn the importance of organic farming in school so that no large company will come and lure them away with its attractive and easy farming methods that promise quick cash. The community also makes small, high-quality chocolate bars so that the local people with meager means can afford to buy the nourishing chocolate themselves and give it to their children.

At Kallari, the entire manufacturing process, from bean to chocolate, is done by hand. The final product, the bars, come in different flavors and sizes. Among others, there is a smaller chocolate bar called Sacha in four varieties including wild cinnamon (72%) and one flavored with chili (75%). The latter has a perfect balance between the chocolate and the chili's heat, which otherwise would dominate the flavor. The most common Kallari bars on the market are the larger ones recognizable by their black labels with a colorful cacao leaf that looks like a feather. Different colored leaves indicate the cacao content: red (70%), green (75%), and blue (85%).

In 2004, Kallari gained the attention of the Slow Food movement in Italy. In 2005, cooperation began with Felchlin in Switzerland—one of the world's best chocolate makers—and the first chocolate bar was produced. In 2010, Kallari began selling chocolate in large parts of Europe. Today, the cooperative shares its factory in Quito with other manufacturers, but it plans to open its own super-modern organic factory in the Napo region in 2013.

THE FAMILY COMPANY PACARI

It was when I met Pacari's founder and owner, Santiago Peralta, at the Ecuadorean embassy in Stockholm a few years ago that I decided to visit the cacao regions of Ecuador in Amazonas.

On the final day of my trip to Ecuador, I traveled to Quito in order to visit Pacari, whose name means "nature" in the native language of the Kichwa. It is a family-owned company both started and owned by the married pair Santiago Peralta and Carla Barboto. They work hard to showcase the best characteristics of the arriba bean and make chocolate of the absolute highest quality. They were among the first in the world to work with both "single origin" beans from Ecuador and raw chocolate. Raw means that the chocolate is organic and never heated over 108°F, which means that it retains important enzymes and nutrients. This is a manufacturing process that clearly places a high priority on methods that are both people- and environment-friendly.

Santiago has always been interested in organic farming because his father organically farmed. Lately, he has also been a proponent of biodynamic farming methods, which he has introduced to his company's cacao farmers who follow the biodynamic harvesting calendar and work for biodynamic certification. This has already led to greater and heartier harvests.

Pacari works with about 3,000 cacao farmers, providing an income and ensuring that these farmers' children can get better schooling. Among other projects, Pacari has been involved in project "Flashlamp" which distributes flashlights to thousands of families with children so that they can safely get around in the dark. Santiago is involved in many local social projects that benefit the cacao farmers as well as a lot of biodynamic, international projects.

The little Pacari factory outside Quito produces chocolate sold all over the world. Here, the biggest part of production is done by hand and is carefully controlled by Santiago, who finds himself in the factory almost daily. They make beneficial raw chocolate bars that are in turn flavored with other healthy ingredients, for example, blueberries from the Andes that grow at high altitude, or lemongrass that has antibacterial properties and aids digestion (lemongrass has a long tradition in chocolate making in Ecuador). They produce a chocolate flavored with merkén, a spice blend used by the Mapuche people in Chile to give the chocolate a hot chili, smoky flavor. They also make a chocolate bar that contains nibs and rock salt, and a "green" chocolate with antioxidants in the form of spirulina algae.

The factory produces chocolate flavors that are shaped by regions like Esmeraldas and Manabí. These chocolate bars are influenced by the soil, the climate, and the farming culture. Santiago explained proudly how Pacari's "Esmeraldas 60%" is made; the bean grows where oranges are grown so that the chocolate has a floral, fruity flavor of citrus and caramel tones. Pacari's "Manabí" derives its soft character of mineral tones without bitterness from the volcanic soil.

We also got to try an eight-course meal made with Pacari's chocolate and prepared by one of Quito's star restaurateurs. One of the courses was lamb confit in cacao butter!

HEALTHY CACAO

Research has shown that cacao contains many heart-friendly substances. Cacao has high amounts of flavonoids and antioxidants that protect cells and may even help prevent atherosclerosis, plaque buildup in the arteries.

Raw chocolate contains, among other things, high amounts of iron, zinc, and magnesium. Magnesium helps balance blood pressure and is good for nerve and muscle function, the heart, and the kidneys. Raw chocolate also contains MAO-inhibitors, which stimulate the neurotransmitter serotonin and other neurotransmitters in the brain that produce feel-good emotions.

Cacao butter is believed to be a good disinfectant and has long been used to soothe burns and soften chapped lips, hands, and feet.

Here are a few ways to utilize chocolate's healthy benefits while simultaneously enjoying it!

DESSERT

Make a fruit salad and shave raw chocolate over it, preferably with some other extra nutritious ingredients like spirulina or dried blueberries.

SNACK

A raw chocolate and nut mix is the perfect snack to take with you in a plastic bag. Coarsely chop raw chocolate and blend with nuts and dried energy-rich berries like blueberries, cranberries, or raisins.

SWEETS

Melt and temper raw chocolate (see page 21) and mix with shredded coconut. Place a spoonful on parchment paper and let the chocolate harden. Simple and nutritious sweets!

RAW
CHOCOLATE

ABOUT RAW CHOCOLATE

Without a doubt, it's the "raw" that counts! Because chocolate has undergone successful technical development and industrially adjusted production for years, the focus has now shifted to raw chocolate, small-scale production, organic and fair-trade farming, a careful handling of the raw material, and a gentle manufacturing process.

The critical portions of chocolate manufacturing are the roasting of the bean and its conching. In the case of raw chocolate, the beans are not roasted but dried, and the chocolate is not heated over 122°F. Certain manufacturers handle and heat the beans to only 108–113°F. The advantages of such a low temperature are that the finished chocolate then retains more aromas and many of the nutrients in the cacao bean. Raw chocolate contains high amounts of magnesium, as

well as other substances that influence neurotransmitters in the brain and help us feel good.

When cacao beans are roasted, the flavor is heightened and becomes deeper, more bitter, and more intense, but they also lose many of their aromatic nuances and flavors. This means that 100% raw chocolate can taste really mild yet full-bodied and pleasant, compared with ordinary 100% chocolate that can seem strong and bitter.

When it comes to the grinding of the bean, the chocolate is at its most enjoyable when it is finely ground and so smooth that it melts on the tongue. Certain manufacturers, however, are recently choosing to return to a coarser grinding, which produces a "sandier" consistency and a completely different experience. There are even raw chocolate

varieties that contain crushed cacao beans, which gives the chocolate a lightly acidic flavor. Mulu makes such a crunchy raw chocolate bar with crushed cacao beans. The company even has a dark, smooth, raw chocolate and a milk chocolate (58%) that contains agave syrup and sunflower lecithin (agave is a sweet nectar with low glycemic index, or GI, that is healthier than sugar).

In my recipes, you can easily substitute the chocolate with raw chocolate. The recipes marked with the **RAW** stamp in the raw chocolate chapter are prepared without a high temperature and according to raw food principles.

VEGAN TRUFFLES

These non-dairy chocolate treats are nutritious and refreshing, and as calming as a cup of tea.

40–42 PIECES

7 oz cashew nuts

5 oz (about 2 cups) shredded
   coconut

1¾ oz sesame seeds

2 tbsp cacao powder

1 tbsp agave syrup or honey

3½ oz raw chocolate (70%),
   melted, for rolling

⅔ cup raw cacao powder,
   for rolling

CHOCOLATE TRUFFLES

Soak the nuts in a bowl with cold water and cover with a plate. Let stand at room temperature overnight. Drain the water and put the nuts in a food processor. Add the coconut, sesame seeds, cacao powder, and agave syrup and pulse until a thick paste forms. Roll the batter into balls and coat them first in melted raw chocolate, and then roll them in cacao powder. This gives the balls a protective chocolate shell. It also works well to roll them only in cacao powder or melted chocolate.

40–42 PIECES

7 oz cashew nuts

7 oz (scant 3 cups) shredded
   coconut

Seeds of 1 vanilla bean or 2
   tsp of vanilla extract

3 tbsp of agave syrup or honey

3½ oz raw chocolate (70%),
   melted, for rolling

⅔ cup raw cacao powder,
   for rolling

VANILLA AND COCONUT TRUFFLES

Soak the nuts in a bowl with cold water and cover with a plate. Let stand at room temperature overnight. Drain the water and put the nuts in a food processor. Add the coconut, vanilla seeds, and agave syrup and pulse until a thick paste forms. Roll the mixture into balls and coat them first in the melted raw chocolate and then in the cacao powder. This gives the balls a protective chocolate shell. It also works well to roll them only in cacao powder or melted chocolate.

CHOCOLATE BALLS

ABOUT 20 PIECES

3½ oz raw chocolate (70%),
    divided

3 oz dried figs

3½ oz almond paste

1 tbsp raw cacao powder

40 g (about 3 tbsp) room
    temperature butter

⅔ cup rolled oats

1¾ oz raw chocolate (70%),
    for rolling

½ cup shredded coconut

FIG BALLS

Finely chop half of the raw chocolate and set aside. Rinse the figs, cut off the hard stems, and chop them into small pieces. Place the pieces in a standing mixer along with the almond paste, cacao powder, and butter and mix on medium-high speed until the figs break down and a thick paste forms. Transfer the mixture to a bowl and fold in the oats and chopped raw chocolate. Roll into balls and set them on a dish or a little tray. Place them in the fridge.

Sprinkle coconut over a plate. Chop and melt the remaining raw chocolate on low power in the microwave and cool to room temperature. Take the balls from the fridge. Place a little of the melted chocolate in the palm of your hand and roll the balls first in the chocolate and then in the coconut.

ABOUT 20 PIECES

1 cup cashew nuts

20 dates, pitted

3 tbsp raw cacao powder

½–1 tbsp agave syrup or
    honey

1 tbsp coconut butter

1¾ oz raw chocolate (70%)
    for rolling the balls

½ cup finely chopped
    pistachio nuts or ½ cup
    blended cacao nibs for
    rolling the balls

PISTACHIO AND RAW CHOCOLATE BALLS

Finely chop the cashew nuts in a food processor. Soak the dates in cold water for about 10 minutes; drain and add to the processor. Pulse the dates with the nuts until combined. Add the cacao powder, agave syrup, and coconut butter and mix rapidly until a smooth batter forms. Let it stand in the fridge for approximately 30 minutes. Remove the batter from the fridge and roll into balls; refrigerate until ready to coat.

Chop the raw chocolate, melt it, and cool to room temperature. Place the nuts on a dish. Remove the balls from the fridge. Place a little melted chocolate in the palm of your hand. Roll each ball in your hand until coated in chocolate, and then roll the balls in the chopped pistachios or nibs.

ABOUT 20 PIECES

½ cup pumpkin seeds

½ cup blanched whole
   almonds

5 dates, pitted

3 tbsp raw cacao powder

3½ oz coconut butter

2 tbsp honey

1 tbsp cold coffee

¾–1 cup shredded coconut

1¾ oz chopped raw chocolate
   (70%) for rolling the balls

½ cup shelled hempseeds or
   sesame seeds

RAW CHOCOLATE BALLS WITH HEMPSEEDS

Pulse the pumpkin seeds and almonds in a food processor until finely chopped. Cut the dates into pieces and add them to the processor; pulse until combined. Add the cacao powder and coconut butter and mix rapidly. Transfer the mixture to a bowl and stir in the honey, coffee, and coconut. Roll into balls and place them on a plate or a little tray. Set in the fridge.

Chop the chocolate, melt on low power in the microwave, and cool to room temperature. Remove the balls from the fridge. Place a little melted chocolate in the palm of your hand and roll the balls first in the chocolate and then roll them in the hempseeds or sesame seeds.

CHOCOLATE PIE

A really super pie with lots of fine ingredients that contain minerals, fiber, and antioxidants! Use coconut butter instead of butter for a vegan version.

10 SERVINGS

Crust

6 dried figs

4 dates, pitted

½ cup blanched hazelnuts

⅔ cup pine nuts

2 tbsp coconut butter or butter

1 tbsp raw cacao powder

Filling

⅔ cup coconut cream

10½ oz raw chocolate (70%)

3½ oz mixed dried berries, dried fruit, and nuts (such as cranberries, raisins, Brazil nuts, walnuts, or hazelnuts) or 7 oz fresh berries

1 tbsp millet seeds or puffed quinoa

Stem the figs, cut them into pieces, and soak them for 30 minutes; drain. Cut the dates into pieces. Pulse the figs and dates together in a food processor until they are broken down and transfer them to a large bowl. Put the hazelnuts and pine nuts in the processor, pulse until coarsely ground, and stir them together with the figs and dates in the bowl.

Melt the coconut butter or butter and pour it into the bowl along with the cacao powder. Mix until well combined and press the batter into the bottom and sides of a 9-inch pie plate. Place the crust in the fridge.

Warm the coconut cream to about 104°F, until it is a little more than lukewarm. Melt the chocolate carefully in intervals on low in the microwave, stirring frequently. Remove the pan with the coconut cream from the heat and stir it into the melted chocolate. Let the mixture cool briefly and then pour it into the piecrust. Refrigerate the pie for 3–4 hours until the filling has solidified. Top the pie with dried berries, dried fruit, and nuts or fresh berries and garnish the pie with the millet seeds or puffed quinoa.

VEGAN CHOCOLATE MOUSSE

A perfect vegan dessert packed with nutritious minerals and fiber, energizing raw chocolate, and agave syrup, a natural sweetener with a low GI value.

6 PORTIONS

7 oz cashew nuts

3½ oz pitted prunes

7 oz raw chocolate (70%)

Scant ½ cup coconut cream

1 tbsp agave syrup, or as desired

Garnish

Sesame seeds, cacao nibs, chopped raw chocolate, shredded coconut, or chopped cashews

Soak the nuts and prunes in cold water in separate, sealed bowls at room temperature overnight.

Drain the cashews and prunes. Puree each separately in a food processor and transfer each to a large bowl. Chop the chocolate and melt. Combine the mixed nuts and prunes and coconut cream. Stir in the chocolate and sweeten with agave syrup.

Divide the mousse into glasses and top with sesame seeds, nibs, chocolate, coconut, or cashew nuts.

FIG BARS

These tasty, energy-rich bars are simple to make and great for a quick pick-me-up on the run!

ABOUT 25 BARS

7 oz dried figs

1 tbsp raw cacao powder

2 tbsp cold coffee

1¼ cups granola

3½ oz golden raisins

3½ oz chopped dates

¾ cup rolled oats

6–7 oz raw chocolate or ordinary dark chocolate (70%)

1 tsp coconut oil or butter

Rinse the figs and clip off the hard stems. Finely chop them and place in a standing mixer together with the cacao and coffee and blend. On low speed, mix in the granola and half of the raisins and dates. Transfer the mixture to a bowl and mix in the rest of the raisins, dates, and oats.

Line a 9-inch square cake pan with parchment paper. Place the mixture on the paper and spread it evenly with a spatula. Place the form in the fridge.

Melt the chocolate and coconut oil or butter together in a bowl in intervals on low power in the microwave. Stir a few times so that the mixture melts evenly. Remove the pan from the fridge and cover it with chocolate using an offset spatula to spread the chocolate mixture. Place it back in the refrigerator.

When the chocolate has hardened, it is ready to be cut into bars.

CHOCOLATE BALLS WITH DRIED BLUEBERRIES

Small, wonderful energy balls with tons of antioxidants that help fill you with energy before and after a workout!

ABOUT 25 PIECES

6 tbsp room temperature butter

½ cup raw sugar

1 pinch vanilla powder or 1 tsp vanilla sugar

½ cup dried blueberries

2½ cups rolled oats

2 tbsp raw cacao powder

3 tbsp cold, strong coffee

2 tbsp honey

5 oz raw chocolate (70%) or chili chocolate (70%)

Cream the butter, raw sugar, and vanilla powder together in a bowl. Coarsely chop the blueberries and stir them into the butter mixture along with the oats, cacao powder, coffee, and honey. Roll into balls.

Finely chop the raw chocolate and melt half on low power in the microwave; cool to room temperature. Put the remaining chopped chocolate on a plate. Place a dollop of the melted chocolate in the palm of your hand and roll the balls one at a time, first in the melted chocolate, and then in the chopped chocolate. Place the balls on a tray and set in the fridge.

Once firm, the balls can be kept in an airtight container in the fridge. You can also freeze them.

TIP!! You can also roll the balls in cacao nibs that have been finely crushed in a blender.

CHOCOLATE CAKE WITH DATES

A moist chocolate cake with the flavors of the Middle East.

12 SERVINGS

Butter for the pan

7 oz raw chocolate (70%)

200 g (about 1¾ sticks) butter

5 large eggs, separated

⅔ cup muscovado sugar

Scant ½ cup raw sugar

½ cup finely chopped dates

1 tsp ground cinnamon

Preheat the oven to 350°F. Butter a 9-inch springform pan, and line the bottom with greased parchment paper.

Melt the chocolate together with the butter. Whisk the egg yolks and muscovado sugar in a large bowl until lightened and smooth. In a standing mixer, whip the egg whites until foamy. While whipping, gradually add the raw sugar and beat until the whites hold a firm peak. Stir the chocolate mixture into the whipped egg yolks. Stir in the dates and carefully fold in the egg whites until just combined. Sprinkle the cinnamon over the batter.

Pour the batter into the pan and bake the cake on the center rack of the oven for 35–40 minutes. Let the cake cool and then let stand in the fridge overnight before serving.

CHEESECAKE WITH WALNUT CRUST

You don't have to bake in the oven! Let the cake stand in the fridge a few hours until the chocolate has set.

10 SERVINGS

Crust

1 cup walnut halves (save a few to sprinkle over the cake)

3 large butter cookies or graham crackers

1 tbsp raw sugar

1 tbsp coconut oil or butter

Filling

¾ cup plus 1½ tbsp heavy cream

3 large egg yolks plus 1 large egg white

¼ cup raw sugar

7 oz cream cheese, at room temperature

10½ oz raw chocolate (70%)

2 pinches ground cinnamon

2 pinches ground cardamom

Walnuts for garnish

In a food processor, pulse the nuts, cookies, raw sugar, and oil or butter until finely ground and evenly moistened. Press the crumbs into the bottom of an 8- or 9-inch springform pan.

Whip the cream lightly until soft peaks form. In a large bowl, whisk the egg yolks with the raw sugar until lightened. Add the cream cheese and whisk until very smooth. Chop the chocolate, melt it in the microwave, and let stand until room temperature. In a small bowl, whisk the egg white until very foamy. Fold the chocolate, whipped cream, egg white, and spices into the cream cheese batter and stir gently until smooth and creamy.

Pour the batter into the pan over the crust and let it stand in the fridge overnight. Garnish with some chopped walnuts.

RAW CHOCOLATE BARS WITH SALTED ALMONDS

Here you can use the Spanish Marconi almond, lightly salted and blanched in its own oil, or make your own salted almonds.

3 BARS

10½ oz raw chocolate (70%)

1½ oz salted almonds (Spanish Marconi almonds)

1½ oz golden raisins

2 tsp shelled hempseeds, crushed cocoa nibs, puffed quinoa, or puffed amaranth

Roasted Almonds

1½ oz blanched whole almonds

½ tsp neutral oil, such as sunflower oil

2 pinches salt

Chop the chocolate and temper it (see page 20). Divide the chocolate between three 3½-oz chocolate bar molds (see page 24). Sprinkle the almonds, raisins, and hempseeds evenly over the bars before the chocolate has hardened. Place the forms in the fridge and chill for about 20 minutes. Tap the chocolate bars out of the molds and wrap them in paper. Store in a cool place, 60–65°F.

ROASTED ALMONDS

Roast the almonds in a dry frying pan over low heat, stirring constantly, until just beginning to lightly brown around the edges. Drizzle the oil and salt over the nuts in the pan and pour them out onto a paper towel-lined plate to cool.

BRAZIL NUT PRALINES

The Brazil nut tree is one of the oldest tree species in the Amazons and can grow up to 1,000 years old and 165 feet high.

ABOUT 32 PIECES

Brazil Nut Praliné

1¾ oz Brazil nuts

¼ cup granulated sugar

1 tbsp water

Filling

3–3½ oz raw chocolate (70%)

2½ oz milk chocolate

3 tbsp plus 1 tsp heavy cream

1 tbsp honey

2 tsp room temperature butter

1½ oz Brazil nut praliné

Praline Shell

10½ oz raw chocolate (70%)

10½ oz dark chocolate (70%)

Roast the Brazil nuts in a dry frying pan until lightly golden. Chop them into large pieces. Dissolve the sugar and water in a small saucepan and boil over medium heat, without stirring, until it turns a light caramel color. Fold in the nuts and quickly pour the caramel onto a sheet lined with parchment paper. Let cool. Coarsely chop the praliné, transfer it to a food processor, and pulse until finely ground. (Not all of it will be used, but it's difficult to make a smaller amount.)

Chop the dark and milk chocolate and place in a bowl. Bring the cream and honey to a boil and pour it over the chocolate in the bowl; stir until all the chocolate has melted (carefully melt in the microwave a few seconds if some of the chocolate does not melt). Stir in the butter and blend with a hand mixer until very smooth. Fold in the praliné. Fill a disposable piping bag with the filling and let it cool to room temperature.

During this time, mold the praline shells (see page 24). Pipe in the filling up to 1/16 inch below the edge so that the chocolate has room to seal. Let the pralines stand in the fridge for about 15 minutes. Melt and temper the leftover chocolate from the molding. Remove the molds from the fridge and seal the pralines. Scrape off the excess chocolate. Let cool.

Turn the mold upside down and tap out the pralines.

PISTOLE WITH CARDAMOM & EUCALYPTUS

Pistole (chocolate coins) were one of the earliest chocolate confections that were made in France for, among others, the court. They often used such strong spices that only a licensed pharmacist got to work with them.

6 PIECES

5–7 oz raw chocolate (70%)

6–7 drops eucalyptus oil

2 pinches ground cardamom seeds

1 tsp cacao nibs or bits of raw chocolate

String (common meat string, twine, or other natural fiber string)

Chop and temper the chocolate (see page 20).

Add the eucalyptus drops and mold the mixture in round forms such as the kind usually used for molding lollipops. Sprinkle the tops with cardamom and crushed cacao beans (nibs) or bits of raw chocolate and place the molds in the fridge for about 20 minutes.

To attach string, make a hole on every mold with a wooden skewer before the chocolate has hardened completely. Turn the molds upside down and tap out the chocolate. Thread the string through the hole.

ROASTED RAW CHOCOLATE GRANOLA

Luxurious, well-balanced, and crispy granola.

1 LARGE GLASS CONTAINER

5 oz hazelnuts

1¼ cups plain oat flakes or
  rolled oats

¾ cup spelt flakes or oats

¾ cup whole linseeds

¾ cup sunflower seeds

¾ cup pumpkin seeds

¼ cup canola oil or
  sunflower oil

¼ cup water

¼ cup honey or light corn
  syrup or glucose

¾ cup dried blueberries,
  cranberries, or raisins

5 oz raw chocolate (70% or
  100%), chopped

Preheat the oven to 350°F. Line a baking sheet with parchment paper.

Roast the hazelnuts in a dry frying pan until the thin skins begin to crack. Transfer them to a clean dish towel and rub off the skin.

Stir the oats, seeds, and nuts together and spread them over the tray. Whisk the canola oil, water, and honey together and drizzle the mixture over the granola. Toss the mixture to coat and roast in the middle of the oven for 25–30 minutes. Stir now and then so that the mixture doesn't burn but becomes a light golden brown color. Let the granola cool and then dry, uncovered, on the sheet overnight.

Stir in the dried berries and chopped chocolate.

The granola can be kept at room temperature in jar with a tight lid.

BLUEBERRY PRALINES

An unexpected but lucky combination! To enhance the flavor, add a little extra lemon, as the blueberries themselves aren't that sour.

ABOUT 20 PIECES

Filling

5 oz raw chocolate (70%)

6 tbsp plus 2 tsp heavy cream

1 tsp honey

1 tsp fresh lemon juice

¼ cup blueberry puree (blended and strained blueberries)

1½ tbsp room temperature butter

Praline Shell

9 oz raw chocolate (70%)

7 oz dark chocolate (70%)

Finely chop the chocolate for the filling and place in a bowl. Bring the cream and honey to a boil, pour it over the chocolate, and stir until all the chocolate has melted. Pour the lemon juice in the blueberry puree and then stir the blueberry mixture into the chocolate. Stir in the butter and blend with a hand mixer until very smooth. Fill a disposable piping bag with the filling and let it cool to room temperature. During this time, mold the praline shells (see page 24).

Pipe in the filling up to ¹⁄₁₆ inch below the edge so that there is room to seal them with chocolate. Place the pralines in the fridge and let stand for about 30 minutes. Melt the leftover chocolate from the molding and remove the molds from the fridge. Pour the melted chocolate over the forms and scrape off the excess chocolate. Place back in the fridge. It takes about 30 minutes for the chocolate to harden.

Turn the molds upside down and tap out the pralines.

RAW CHOCOLATE ICE CREAM

Ice cream with crispy praliné made with cacao beans. This ice cream is also delicious with a classic praliné made with hazelnuts.

6–8 PORTIONS

½ vanilla bean

1¼ cups heavy cream

1¼ cups milk

2 tbsp honey

4 oz raw chocolate (70%)

5 large egg yolks

½ cup raw sugar

Praliné with Nibs

3 tbsp raw sugar

2 tbsp water

1¾ oz cacao nibs

Split the vanilla bean lengthwise and scrape out the seeds. Bring the cream, milk, vanilla bean and seeds, and honey to a boil in a stainless steel pot. Remove from heat.

Chop the chocolate and place in a bowl. In another bowl, whisk the egg yolks and raw sugar until fluffy. Remove the vanilla bean from the hot cream. Stir the warm cream and milk into the whipped egg yolks and then pour the liquid back into the pot. While whisking, bring the liquid to a simmer until it reaches 185°F or until the mixture begins to thicken. Remove from heat, pour the liquid over the chopped chocolate, and stir until smooth. Strain the mixture through a fine sieve over a bowl. Let cool. Cover with plastic wrap and let it stand in the fridge, preferably overnight, so that the ice cream matures and the flavor becomes creamy and rich.

Dissolve the raw sugar and water in a small saucepan and cook over medium heat, without stirring, until it turns a light caramel color, and add the nibs. Quickly pour onto a sheet of parchment paper; let cool until hardened and chop or crush it into bits. Freeze the ice cream base in an ice cream maker according to manufacturer's instructions until creamy and firm. Fold in the praliné mixture, then transfer the ice cream to an airtight container and freeze for at least 1 hour before serving.

FROZEN TERRINE WITH RASPBERRY GRANITÉ

This is one of my favorite desserts: a smooth, cool, and creamy terrine with a bold chocolate flavor that gets an extra push from the tart raspberry granité.

10 PORTIONS

5 oz raw chocolate (70%)

3½ oz dark chocolate (64%)

125 g (about 1 stick plus 1 tbsp) room temperature butter

¼ cup honey

3 large eggs, separated

Raspberry Granité

8 oz frozen raspberries

½ cup water

¼ cup granulated sugar

½ cup red wine

Garnish

14 oz fresh raspberries

Chop the chocolate and melt it along with the butter and honey over a water bath or in the microwave. Beat the egg yolks and egg whites separately. Remove the chocolate from the heat and let cool slightly. Whisk in the egg yolks and quickly fold in the egg whites. Pour the chocolate mixture in a terrine mold or loaf pan lined with plastic wrap and freeze at least 5 hours or overnight.

Put the raspberries and water into a small saucepan and heat over medium-low heat, without boiling, until the raspberries are very soft. Drain them in a sieve over a bowl. Combine the juice with sugar and red wine. Let it stand in the freezer overnight.

Remove the bowl and scrape the surface of the ice with a fork until fluffy or pulse pieces of the ice in an electric mixer (let it stand about 5 minutes at room temperature first). Slice the terrine and serve it ice cold with the raspberry granité and the fresh raspberries over the top.

CACAO POWDER

Cacao powder is obtained by extracting cacao butter from the cacao mass, drying the residual cacao, and grinding it to a fine powder. There are many different types of cacao powder, distinguished by taste, as well as color, that range from yellow-brown to dark reddish-brown. There is also raw cacao powder, which contains high amounts of nutritious and vital nutrients.

SPONGE CAKE WITH CHOCOLATE

A truly luxurious, filled, rich cake that goes well with a glass of cold milk!

12 SERVINGS

Cake

Butter for the pan

Flour for the pan

2 large eggs

¾ cup granulated sugar

¼ cup muscovado sugar

100 g (about 7 tbsp) butter

½ cup milk

2 tbsp strong cold coffee

4 tbsp cacao powder

2 tsp vanilla sugar

1 tsp baking powder

1¼ cups all-purpose flour

Filling

4 oz dark chocolate (64–70%)

6 tbsp plus 2 tsp heavy cream

2 tbsp room temperature
   butter

Set the oven to 350°F. Butter and flour an 8-cup tube pan.

Whisk the eggs, sugar, and muscovado sugar until lightened and fluffy. Melt the butter in a pot and pour in the milk and coffee. Combine the dry ingredients in a bowl. Alternately add the liquid and dry ingredients to the whipped eggs and stir gently until combined. Pour the batter into the pan and bake in the center of the oven for approximately 50 minutes. Test with a toothpick to see if the cake is ready. Remove the cake and let it rest in the pan for 5 minutes. Invert the cake onto a plate and let it cool under the pan.

Chop the chocolate and put it in a bowl. Bring the cream to a boil. Remove from the heat and pour it over the chocolate, stirring until completely melted. Whisk in the butter until melted and smooth; cool to room temperature.

Divide the sponge cake horizontally through the center with a serrated slicer. Spread or pipe the filling over the bottom half. Replace the top half of the cake. Let the cake stand in a cool place before slicing.

CHOCOLATE MUD CAKE

Chocolate mud cake pairs nicely with lightly whipped cream or either vanilla or chocolate ice cream. Dust with cacao powder, chopped chocolate, or nibs. The licorice version goes well with vanilla ice cream or either raspberry or mango sorbet.

10 SERVINGS

Butter and flour for the pan
2 large eggs
1¼ cups granulated sugar
100 g (about 7 tbsp) butter
1 tsp vanilla sugar
4 tbsp cacao powder
Heaping ¾ cup all-purpose flour

10 SERVINGS

¾ cup granulated sugar
½ cup muscovado sugar
1¾ oz dark chocolate (54–70%)

10 SERVINGS

2 tsp powdered licorice

Icing

2½ oz dark chocolate (70%), chopped
⅓ cup heavy cream
1 tsp powdered licorice

BASE RECIPE

Preheat the oven to 400°F. Butter and flour an 8-inch springform pan. Whisk the eggs and sugar together in a bowl until lightened but not fluffy. Melt and stir in the butter. Add all the dry ingredients and stir well to combine. Pour the batter into the pan and bake on the lowest rack in the oven for 15 minutes. Remove the cake and let it cool at least 1 hour.

WITH MUSCOVADO SUGAR

Prepare in the same way as the chocolate mud cake but use ¾ cup granulated sugar and add the muscovado sugar. While the cake cools, chop and melt the chocolate on low power in the microwave. Drizzle the chocolate over the cake.

WITH LICORICE

Prepare in the same way as the ordinary chocolate mud cake but add powdered licorice to the whipped eggs. While the cake cools, chop the chocolate and place in a bowl. Boil the cream and powdered licorice together, pour it over the chocolate, and stir until melted, then drizzle the chocolate icing over the cake. Dust with a little powdered licorice when the icing has hardened.

MOCHA SQUARES

A classic soft brownie; perfect for coffee breaks.

ABOUT 35 PIECES

Cake

300 g (about 2 sticks plus 5 tbsp) butter

4 large eggs

2½ cups granulated sugar

3¾ cups all-purpose flour

5 tsp baking powder

4 tsp vanilla sugar

4 tbsp cacao powder

1¼ cups milk

Icing

125 g (about 1 stick plus 1 tbsp) butter

8 tbsp cold coffee

3 cups powdered sugar

1 tbsp cacao

4 tsp vanilla sugar

Garnish

3–4 tbsp shredded coconut

Preheat the oven to 350°F. Melt the butter. Whisk the eggs and sugar until fluffy. Combine all the dry ingredients and fold into the whisked eggs together with the butter. Pour in the milk and beat until the batter is smooth.

Pour the batter into a rectangular 11 x 15-inch cake pan, lined with parchment paper. Bake in the center of the oven for 30–35 minutes. Remove the cake and let cool.

Melt the butter and add in the coffee. Let the mixture cool and then whisk in the powdered sugar, cacao powder, and vanilla sugar. Whip until the icing is smooth and spread it over the cake with an offset spatula. Garnish with coconut.

When the chocolate has hardened the cake is ready to be sliced.

RYE BREAD WITH CACAO

This bread has a mild accent of cacao powder and goes well with mild cheeses. Try with apple, apricot, blackberry, or fig jam. Note: In Scandinavia there is a tradition of baking with "scalded" flour.

2 LOAVES

Scalding

1 cup crushed wheat (bulgur)

¼ cup crushed linseeds

1½ tbsp salt

1½ cups boiling hot water

Dough

1¾ oz fresh yeast

1⅔ cups lukewarm water (98.6°F)

¾ cup dark corn syrup or glucose

¾ cup sunflower seeds

¾ cup pumpkin seeds

2½ tbsp cacao powder

2½ cups coarse rye flour

1¾–2 cups whole wheat flour

Butter for the pans

Wheat bran or flour for the pan

Combine all the dry ingredients for the scalded dough in a bowl. Pour in the hot water and stir until the liquid is absorbed. Cover with plastic wrap and let stand at room temperature overnight.

Crumble the yeast in a bowl and pour in the water and syrup. Stir in the scalding mixture, sunflower seeds, pumpkin seeds, cacao powder, and rye flour. Work in the wheat flour, a little at a time, until the dough holds together; knead the dough in the bowl for about 10 minutes.

Preheat the oven to 500°F. Butter two rectangular bread pans and lightly dust them with bran or flour. Divide the fairly soggy dough between the pans. Dust with a little rye flour, cover with a dish towel, and let rise at room temperature for about 30 minutes.

Place the bread in the oven on the lowest rack and lower the temperature to 400°F. Bake on the lowest rack for about 1 hour (eventually cover with aluminum foil for the final 10 minutes). Remove the bread and let the loaves stand in the pans for 5 minutes. Turn out the bread and let it cool, uncovered, on a rack.

CHOCOLATE COOKIE SLICES

These simple and quick cookies make the perfect gift. Wrap them in cellophane and decorate with a ribbon, or place them in an attractive tin.

ABOUT 34 PIECES

175 g (about 1½ sticks) room
  temperature butter
1 cup granulated sugar
1 tbsp vanilla sugar
1½ tbsp cacao powder
1½ cups all-purpose flour
2 tsp baking powder

Preheat the oven to 350°F. Cream the butter, sugar, and vanilla sugar together in a bowl. Combine the rest of the ingredients and then fold them into the creamed butter and sugar; beat until the dough is smooth.

Divide the dough and press each piece into a long rectangle. Set them on a baking sheet lined with parchment paper and press the dough out with your fingers, preserving the rectangular shape, until it is about ¼-inch thick. Bake in the center of the oven for 12–15 minutes.

Remove the cookies. Cut them into about ¾-inch-wide pieces.

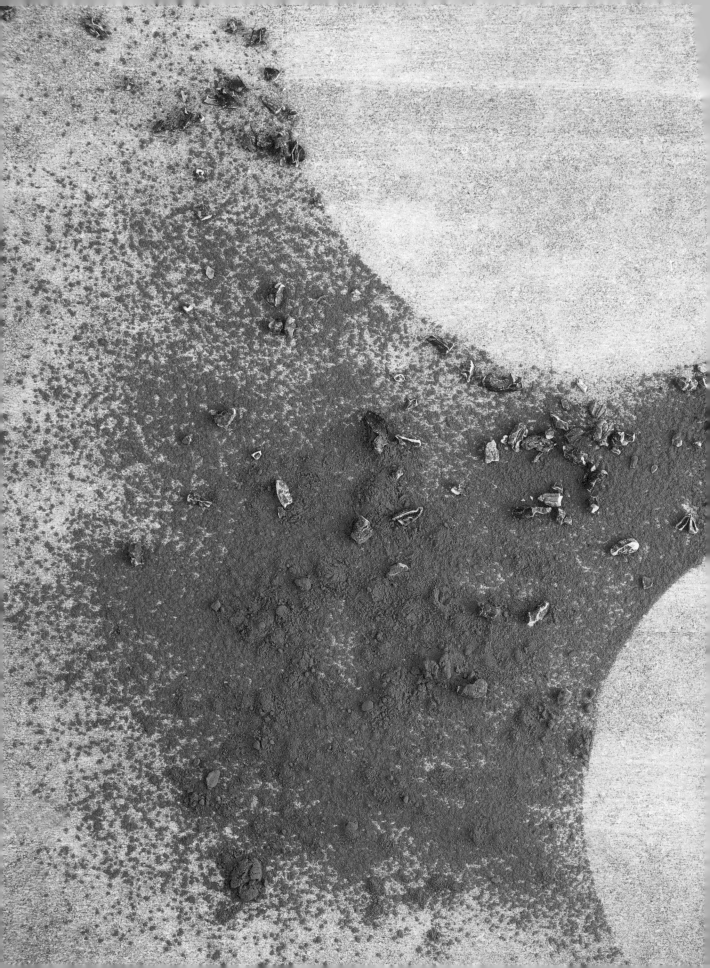

SOFT CAKES & COOKIES

BAKLAVA

Baklava is a sweet, classic cookie that is served with tea in the Middle East. This version has a wonderful chocolate filling that goes well with Greek or Turkish yogurt flavored with ground cardamom seeds.

1 PAN, 24 PIECES

Cookie

5 oz walnut halves

4 oz shelled pistachios

7 oz dark chocolate (64–70%)
   or chocolate chips

7 oz almond paste

60 g (about 4 tbsp) room
   temperature butter

¼ cup granulated sugar

2 tsp vanilla sugar

1 tsp ground cinnamon

½ tsp ground cardamom

2 large eggs

1 tbsp all-purpose flour

1 tbsp cacao powder

100 g (about 7 tbsp) butter

15 sheets of phyllo dough,
   preferably Greek, preferably
   9 x 13 inches in diameter

Honey Topping

½ cup water

½ cup granulated sugar

2 tbsp honey

Finely grated zest and juice
   of ½ lemon or orange

Preheat the oven to 325°F. Finely chop the walnuts and pistachios by hand or in a food processor. Set aside. Chop the chocolate. Grate the almond paste and put it into a bowl. Add the butter, sugar, vanilla sugar, cinnamon, cardamom, and eggs and mix on low speed until combined and smooth. Stir the flour, nuts, and chocolate into the batter along with the cacao powder until combined.

Brush the bottom of an 8 x 12-inch cake pan, with melted butter and line with a sheet of phyllo dough. Brush 5 sheets of phyllo dough with melted butter and layer them in the bottom of the pan. Spread two-thirds of the nut filling over the dough. Continue by brushing and layering another 5 sheets of phyllo dough. Spread the remaining ⅓ of the nut mixture on top. Complete with a final 5 sheets of phyllo dough, brushing all the layers, including the surface of the topmost layer, with butter. Using a sharp knife, score the top layer into squares about 2 inches in diameter. Bake in the oven for 40–50 minutes until the baklava turns a light golden-brown color.

Make the honey drizzle by blending all the ingredients in a pot and boiling until it reaches 225°F. Strain. When the baklava has cooled, pour the syrup gently over the top and let stand until liquid is absorbed before slicing.

BROWNIES

Soft, rich, and a little chewy. . . serve with a dollop of lightly whipped cream or vanilla ice cream. Delicious!

ABOUT 20 SQUARES

4½ oz dark chocolate (58–64%)

100 g (about 7 tbsp) room temperature butter

1¼ cups granulated sugar

2 large eggs

2 tbsp cacao powder

1 tsp vanilla sugar

Scant ½ cup all-purpose flour

3½ oz white or dark chocolate (70%)

3½ oz pecans or walnuts

Preheat the oven to 350°F. Chop the 4½ oz of dark chocolate and melt on low power in the microwave; cool to room temperature. Cream the butter and the sugar together by hand or in a standing mixer. Whisk the eggs in a separate bowl. Fold the whipped eggs into the sugar and butter a little at a time (this will cause the surface of the brownie to crack and become crisp), and then add the melted chocolate. Sift the cacao powder, vanilla sugar, and flour together and gently fold into the batter.

Coarsely chop the white or remaining dark chocolate and nuts and fold them into the chocolate batter. Line the bottom of a 9-inch square cake pan with parchment paper. Pour in the batter and bake for 27–30 minutes. When the brownies are ready they will still be a little soft in the middle.

Let cool and cut into squares.

FUDGE BROWNIES

This rich brownie, with a fudgy consistency, is creamy and soft from baking at a low temperature.

ABOUT 25 SQUARES

Cookie

200 g (about 1¾ sticks) butter

1⅔ cups granulated sugar

4 large eggs

1¼ cups cacao powder

1 tsp vanilla sugar

2 tsp instant coffee

1 tsp baking powder

1¼ cups all-purpose flour

Icing

5 oz dark chocolate (56–70%)

⅔ cup powdered sugar

⅓ cup cacao powder

100 g (about 7 tbsp) room
    temperature butter

2 tbsp hot coffee

1–2 tbsp chopped cacao nibs

Preheat the oven to 300°F. Melt the butter and the sugar together in a bowl. In a large bowl, whisk the eggs, cacao powder, vanilla sugar, instant coffee, and baking powder together until combined; stir in the melted butter. Fold in the flour. Pour the batter into a 9 x 11-inch rectangular pan lined with parchment paper. Bake the brownies for 20 minutes at 300°F and then increase the heat to 350°F and bake for another 5 minutes.

Remove the brownies and cool to room temperature. Chop the chocolate and melt over a water bath or in the microwave. Cream the powdered sugar, cacao powder, and butter together in a bowl, and stir in the coffee and the melted chocolate. Spread the icing over the brownies and let stand until it cools to room temperature. Garnish with cacao nibs and slice into squares.

CHOCOLATE CHEESECAKE

The Rolls-Royce of cheesecakes! A striking crust with a creamy, chocolate filling.

14 SERVINGS

Crust

200 g (about 1¾ sticks) room temperature butter

1 cup granulated sugar

1 tsp vanilla sugar

1¼ cups all-purpose flour

½ cup cacao powder

Butter for the pan

Filling

7 oz dark chocolate (70%)

10½ oz cream cheese, at room temperature

3 large eggs, at room temperature

¼ cup granulated sugar

1 tsp vanilla sugar

¾ cup plus 1½ tbsp heavy cream, at room temperature

2 tbsp cooled espresso coffee (or strongly made coffee)

½ tbsp cacao powder

In a standing mixer, cream the butter, sugar, vanilla sugar, flour, and cacao powder together on low until thick and smooth. Line the bottom of a 9-inch springform pan with parchment paper, and butter the sides of the pan. Pour the batter into the pan and smooth out the surface; refrigerate.

Preheat the oven to 350°F. Chop the chocolate and melt it in the microwave on low power, stirring it every so often so that it doesn't burn. In a standing mixer, cream the cream cheese, eggs, sugar, and vanilla sugar until very smooth. Add the melted chocolate, cream, and coffee and mix on low until combined and very smooth.

Remove the pan from the fridge and pour in the filling. Bake the cake in the center of the oven for about 55 minutes.

Remove from the oven and let cool to room temperature. Place in the fridge for at least 2–3 hours. Garnish the top with a dusting of cacao powder before serving.

FUDGE CAKE

This wonderful cake is covered with a soft, chocolate-caramel icing. Serve with a dollop of lightly whipped cream or a scoop of ice cream with fresh berries.

12 SERVINGS

Cake

Butter for the pan
150 g (about 1¼ stick) butter
2 large eggs
1 cup granulated sugar
1 tsp vanilla sugar
1 tbsp cold coffee
⅔ cup all-purpose flour
1¼ cups cacao powder
1 tsp baking powder

Fudge

3½ oz dark chocolate
   (64–70%)
⅔ cup heavy cream
⅔ cup granulated sugar
2 tbsp dark corn syrup or
   glucose
5 tbsp room temperature
   butter

Preheat the oven to 350°F. Butter a 9-inch springform pan.

Melt the butter in a bowl. Whisk the eggs, sugar, and vanilla sugar together until lightened. Add the coffee. Sift the flour, cacao powder, and baking powder together and fold into the eggs; stir in the melted butter. Distribute the batter evenly in the pan and place in the center of the oven. Bake for about 20 minutes. Remove the cake and let it cool.

Chop the chocolate and put into a saucepan with the cream, sugar, and corn syrup or glucose. Bring the mixture to a boil and cook until it thickens and has become glossy. Continually stir, making sure to stir all the way to the bottom. Remove the pan from the heat and stir in the butter. Let the fudge cool slightly so that it reaches a thicker consistency.

Pour the fudge over the chocolate cake and spread it evenly with an offset spatula. Let cool.

IMPORTANT!! Let the cake stand for 5 hours or overnight in the fridge.

CHILI CHOCOLATE CAKE

For an extra spicy kick, you can use chili chocolate (64–70%) in the icing.

12-14 SERVINGS

Crust

Butter for the pan

Flour for the pan

14 oz dark chocolate (56–70%)

100 g (about 7 tbsp) butter

4 large eggs

1¼ cups granulated sugar

Heaping ¾ cup all-purpose flour

½–1 fresh red chili

Chocolate Icing

3½ oz dark chocolate (64–70%)

6 tbsp plus 2 tsp heavy cream

1 tbsp light corn syrup or glucose

2 tsp room temperature butter

Preheat the oven to 350°F. Butter a 9-inch springform pan and flour it lightly. Chop the chocolate and melt it together with the butter over a water bath or in a microwave. Whisk the eggs and sugar together until lightened but not fluffy. Combine the chocolate mixture with the eggs and fold in the flour. Chop the chili and stir into the batter. Pour the batter into the pan and bake in the center of the oven for about 25 minutes. Remove and let cool.

Chop the chocolate and place in a bowl. Bring the cream and syrup to a boil and pour it over the chocolate, stirring until all the chocolate has melted.

Whisk the butter into the chocolate until smooth and spread the chocolate icing over the cake.

CHOCOLATE CAKE WITH GREEN TEA

Matcha is a fine green tea powder made from the best tea leaves and goes well with dark chocolate. It can be a little bitter, so it's important not to use too much.

20 PIECES

Butter for the pan

Flour for the pan

150 g (about 1¼ sticks) room
   temperature butter

1 tbsp vanilla sugar

¾ cup granulated sugar

6 oz dark chocolate (70%)

3 large eggs, separated

⅔ cup all-purpose flour

2 pinches salt

1 tbsp green tea powder
   (Matcha powder)

Preheat the oven to 350°F. Butter a 9-inch square pan, preferably with a removable bottom, and dust it lightly with flour. You can also line it with parchment paper.

In a standing mixer, whip the butter, vanilla sugar, and sugar together until lightened and fluffy. Chop the chocolate and melt in the microwave. Beat the egg whites in a separate bowl. Stir the egg yolks into the butter mixture and then whisk in the chocolate. Fold in the flour, salt, and egg whites. Pour the batter into the pan and bake on the lowest rack for about 25 minutes.

Remove and let cool. When the cake is completely cool and firm, dust it with Matcha powder and cut into pieces.

SOUTH AFRICAN MUD CAKE

This cake contains a lot of liquid, which makes it extra moist. It works well as a dessert on a buffet because it can sit out without becoming dry.

12 SERVINGS

Butter for the pan

5 oz dark chocolate (70%)

1⅔ cups all-purpose flour

1 tsp baking soda

1 pinch salt

2 tsp vanilla sugar

1 cup strong coffee

¼ cup whiskey

160 g (about 1 stick plus 3 tbsp)
    room temperature butter

1¼ cups granulated sugar

2 large eggs

Sauce

½ cup granulated sugar

2 tbsp butter

½ cup heavy cream

1 large egg yolk

2 tbsp milk

1 tbsp whiskey

Preheat the oven to 300°F. Butter a 2-quart loaf pan.

Chop the chocolate. Combine the flour, baking soda, salt, and vanilla sugar. Warm the coffee and whiskey over a water bath and add the chocolate and butter. Stir until the chocolate and butter is melted and smooth.

Remove the bowl from the water bath and stir in the sugar. Let the mixture cool for 5 minutes. Pour the batter into a standing mixer and on low speed, slowly add the dry ingredients a little at a time. You can also use a handheld stick blender. Add the eggs and mix until combined. Pour the batter into the pan and bake for about 55 minutes. Let the cake stand in a cool place for several hours, preferably overnight, so that it has time to set.

WHISKEY-CARAMEL SAUCE

Melt the sugar and butter in a saucepan over medium heat and continue cooking, stirring frequently, until it turns a light caramel. Carefully add the cream and let the sauce boil a few minutes. Whisk the egg yolk, milk, and whiskey together; remove the pan from the heat and quickly whisk in the egg mixture.

Slice the cake and drizzle the sauce over it. This cake is great with fresh strawberries and a dollop of cream on the side.

CHOCOLATE & RED BEET CAKE

Robust red beets and dark chocolate make this cake a real delicacy. For a spicy flavor, use a dark chili chocolate.

10 SERVINGS

Cake

Butter and flour for the pan
2 large eggs
Heaping ¾ cup raw sugar
Heaping ¾ cup all-purpose flour
1 tsp baking powder
1 tsp baking soda
1 tsp vanilla sugar
1 tsp ground cinnamon
⅓ cup sunflower oil
1¼ cups peeled and coarsely
    grated red beets
3½ oz dark chocolate (68–70%)
1¾ oz hazelnuts

Icing

5 oz softened cream cheese
50 g (about 3½ tbsp) room
    temperature butter
⅔ cup powdered sugar
1 tsp vanilla sugar
1 tbsp milk

Garnish

Chopped chocolate
Chopped hazelnuts

Preheat the oven to 350°F. Butter and flour a 9-inch springform pan.

Whisk the eggs and raw sugar together until lightened. Combine the flour, baking powder, baking soda, vanilla sugar, and cinnamon together and fold it into the whisked eggs along with the oil and beets.

Coarsely chop the chocolate and nuts (save a little for garnishing), and fold them into the batter. Pour the batter into the pan and bake in the center of the oven for 35–40 minutes. Let the cake cool.

In a standing mixer, whip the cream cheese, butter, powdered sugar, and vanilla sugar together until smooth and creamy, adding the milk at the end. Ice the cooled cake with the icing and sprinkle the chopped chocolate and nuts over the top.

MOUSSE CAKE WITH COFFEE & CHOCOLATE

Try this with a glass of homemade coffee liqueur (see page 237).

16 SERVINGS

Crust

18 oz almond paste

5 large egg whites (save the
yolks for the filling)

Optional 1 tbsp all-purpose
flour

Filling

12 oz dark chocolate (54–68%)

1⅔ cups heavy cream

4 large egg yolks

2 tbsp cold espresso coffee

Garnish

½ tsp cacao powder

1 tbsp coffee beans

Preheat the oven to 350°F. Trace two circles, about 9 inches in diameter, on two pieces of parchment paper and place each one on a baking sheet.

In a standing mixer, beat the almond paste with one of the egg whites until softened and liquefied. In another bowl, whisk the remaining egg whites until soft peaks form. Fold the whites into the almond paste, gradually sift in the flour, and fold gently until just combined. Divide the batter and spread it within the traced circles. Bake the disks in the center of the oven for about 18 minutes. Let cool.

Chop the chocolate and melt it over a water bath or on low power in a microwave. Lightly whip the cream until soft peaks form. Remove the chocolate from the water bath and quickly whisk in the egg yolks, one at a time. Fold in the coffee and cream in three batches, working quickly.

Place one of the egg white disks into the bottom of a 9-inch springform pan. Pour in half of the mousse and then place the other disk on top of the mousse. Fill with the rest of the mousse. Let stand in the fridge for about 4–5 hours until the mousse is firm and set.

Dust the cake with cacao powder and garnish with coffee beans.

SMALL COOKIES, PIES & PASTRIES

CHOCOLATE COOKIES

5 oz dark chocolate (64–70%)

3½ oz walnut halves or pecans

225 g (about 2 sticks) room
temperature butter

1 cup muscovado sugar or
raw sugar

¾ cup granulated sugar

2 large eggs

1 tsp vanilla sugar

2½ cups all-purpose flour

¼ cup cacao powder

1 tsp baking powder

DARK COOKIES

Preheat the oven to 350°F. Chop the chocolate and nuts and set aside. In a standing mixer, cream the butter, muscovado or raw sugar, and granulated sugar together until smooth; add the eggs and vanilla sugar and mix well. Combine the flour, cacao powder, and baking powder and fold into the egg batter. Add the chocolate and nuts and mix well. Divide the batter into 25 portions and roll them into balls. Place the balls on a baking sheet lined with parchment paper, flatten them lightly, and bake for 12–15 minutes. Cool the cookies on a rack.

ABOUT 25 COOKIES

225 g (about 2 sticks) room
temperature butter

1 cup packed brown sugar

¾ cup granulated sugar

2 large eggs

1 tsp vanilla sugar

2¾ cups all-purpose flour

1 tsp baking powder

5 oz dark chocolate (54–65%),
coarsely chopped or chips

LIGHT COOKIES

Preheat the oven to 350°F. In a standing mixer, cream the butter, brown sugar, and granulated sugar together until smooth; add the eggs and vanilla sugar and mix well. Combine the flour and baking powder and stir it into the butter mixture. Fold in the chocolate. Divide the batter into 25 portions and roll them into balls. Place the balls on a baking sheet lined with parchment paper, flatten them lightly, and bake for 12–15 minutes. Cool the cookies on a rack.

ABOUT 25 COOKIES

5 oz milk chocolate

5 oz salted or unsalted peanuts

225 g (about 2 sticks) room
temperature butter

1 cup light muscovado sugar
or raw sugar

¾ cup granulated sugar

2 large eggs

1 tsp vanilla sugar

2¾ cups all-purpose flour

1 tsp baking powder

PEANUT COOKIES

Preheat the oven to 350°F. Chop the chocolate and nuts
and set aside. In a standing mixer, cream the butter,
muscovado or raw sugar, and granulated sugar together
until smooth; add the eggs and vanilla sugar and mix
well. Combine the flour and baking powder and fold
into the creamed butter; stir in the chocolate and nuts.
Divide the batter into 25 portions and roll them into
balls. Place the balls on a baking sheet lined with
parchment paper, flatten them lightly, and bake for
12–15 minutes. Cool the cookies on a rack.

CHOCOLATE FONDANT

A creamy chocolate dessert served either on a plate or in a cup.

8 PORTIONS

200 g (about 1¾ sticks) room
    temperature butter

½ cup granulated sugar

7 oz dark chocolate (64–70%)

4 large whole eggs

4 large egg yolks

7 tbsp all-purpose flour

Preheat the oven to 400°F. Cream the butter and sugar together in a bowl with a rubber spatula or spoon. Chop the chocolate, melt it in the microwave, and cool slightly; stir it into the creamed butter.

Whisk the eggs and egg yolks well in another bowl and combine the whipped eggs with the chocolate batter. Fold in the flour and divide the mixture between buttered ramekins or heat-resistant cappuccino cups. Bake in the center of the oven for 8–10 minutes.

The fondant can be eaten directly from the cups or can be carefully inverted onto a plate. In either case, let it sit in the dish or cup for 2 minutes before serving.

Serve with ice cream and lightly whipped cream.

CHOCOLATE MERINGUES

Make these meringues even better by topping with chopped peanuts or hazelnuts before placing them in the oven.

ABOUT 30 PIECES

1 cup egg whites

2¼ cups granulated sugar

2½ oz dark chocolate (64–70%)

Optional chopped peanuts or hazelnuts

Preheat the oven to 265°F. Whisk the egg whites and sugar in a stainless steel bowl.

Place the bowl over a water bath (a pot with about 2 inches of boiling water) and whisk the meringue until it forms stiff peaks. The temperature of the mixture should be 130–140°F. Remove the bowl from the water bath and beat the meringue with an electric mixer until it cools to room temperature.

Chop the chocolate and melt it on low power in the microwave. Fold it into the meringue briefly so that the batter becomes marbled; do not overmix.

Using two large spoons, heap the meringue into 30 portions onto a baking sheet lined with parchment paper. Top with chopped nuts. Bake in the center of the oven for 35–40 minutes. When ready, the meringues will be a little chewy inside.

CHOCOLATE MAZARINES WITH CHERRIES

Tender, moist, and striking miniature tarts! Use an olive pitter to remove the cherry pits prior to decorating.

ABOUT 20 PORTIONS

Pie Shell

200 g (about 1¾ sticks) butter

1 tsp vanilla sugar

½ cup granulated sugar

Scant 2 cups all-purpose flour

2 tbsp cacao powder

Filling

7 oz dark chocolate (56–64%)

7 oz almond paste

50 g (about 3½ tbsp) room
  temperature butter

¼ cup granulated sugar

1 tbsp all-purpose flour

1 tbsp cacao powder

½ tsp baking powder

1 large egg

Individual ovensafe paper
  brioche molds or sturdy
  cupcake liners

Garnish

1¾ cups pitted fresh cherries

Preheat the oven to 350°F. Beat the butter, vanilla sugar, and granulated sugar with an electric mixer until creamy. Add the flour and cacao powder and mix on low until a crumbly dough forms. Squeeze the dough together with your fingers and set it on a lightly floured surface. Divide the dough and roll each half to about 1½–2 inches thick. Cut each half into 10 portions, about 1⅛ inches thick. Press the dough into the brioche molds evenly to create a crust.

Chop the chocolate and set it aside. Put the almond paste in a standing mixer and mix on low until broken down and smooth. Add the butter, sugar, flour, cacao powder combined with the baking powder, egg, and chocolate and mix well until combined and smooth. Divide the filling between the dough-lined paper molds. Decorate each cake with 2–3 cherries.

Bake the cakes in the center of the oven for 25–30 minutes until they turn light golden brown.

CHOCOLATE DOUGHNUTS

Easier to make than you might think! Choose between round, filled and sugar-coated balls, or chocolate-topped rings.

ABOUT 60 DOUGHNUTS

Doughnuts

1¾ oz fresh yeast

150 g (about 1¼ sticks) butter

2 cups plus 2 tbsp milk

½ cup granulated sugar

½ tsp salt

6⅓–6¾ cups flour

1¼ cups granulated sugar,
    for tossing

Neutral oil, such as canola,
    for frying

Chocolate Filling

4 oz dark chocolate (70%)

6 tbsp plus 2 tsp heavy cream

1 tbsp corn syrup or honey or
    glucose

Chocolate Glaze

7 oz dark chocolate (64–70%)

Crumble the yeast in a bowl. Melt the butter in a saucepan, add the milk, and heat until lukewarm, about 98°F. Pour the liquid over the yeast and stir. Stir in the sugar and salt and work in the flour a little at a time. Knead the dough gently in the bowl for about 5 minutes and then roll it out on a lightly floured surface until flat, about ½ inch thick. Punch out the doughnuts with a round doughnut or cookie cutter and make a hole in the middle of each doughnut (if you're making filled doughnuts, then do not punch this center hole in the doughnut).

Pour the sugar on a dish. Let the doughnuts rise about 10 minutes. Fry them until light brown in 350°F oil. Remove them from the oil and let them drain quickly on a rack or paper towels. Roll the doughnuts that will be filled with chocolate filling in the sugar.

Chop the chocolate coarsely and place in a bowl. Bring the cream and corn syrup or honey to a boil and pour it over the chocolate. Stir until all the chocolate has melted. Fill a disposable piping bag with the filling and let cool to room temperature. Pipe the filling into the doughnuts when they have cooled.

To glaze the doughnuts, melt the chocolate and dip the doughnut rings on one side.

PAIN AU CHOCOLAT

It can be a little tricky making rolled dough, but it is absolutely worth the trouble! For a shortcut, use ready-made puff pastry.

ABOUT 30 PORTIONS

Dough

1 batch of Danish dough
(see page 132 recipe for
Chocolate Danish) or
ready-made puff pastry

Filling

3½ oz dark chocolate or
chocolate chips (64–70%)

1¾ oz Nutella (hazelnut
spread)

1 large egg, for brushing

3 tbsp raw sugar

Preheat the oven to 425°F. Chop the chocolate and set aside.

Roll out the dough and cut into 30 rectangular portions, about 2½ x 5 inches. Spread Nutella in a line down the middle of each flattened dough piece, sprinkle the chocolate over the Nutella, and roll the widest side of the dough tightly into a cylinder. Place seam-side down on a baking sheet lined with parchment paper.

Brush the rolls with lightly whisked egg and sprinkle raw sugar over the top. Score the top of each roll with three cuts using a sharp knife. Bake in the center of the oven for 5–10 minutes until the dough turns a nice golden brown color.

SHORTBREAD WITH PECANS & CHOCOLATE

The basis of this recipe is a classic and really good shortbread recipe— I have added pecans and chocolate. The cookies pair well with coffee, tea, or ice cream.

40 PORTIONS

3½ oz pecans

3½ oz dark chocolate (56–70%)

Heaping 2 cups all-purpose flour

200 g (about 1¾ sticks) room temperature butter

½ cup granulated sugar

2 large egg yolks

2 tsp vanilla sugar

Preheat the oven to 350°F. Chop the nuts and chocolate and set aside. In a standing mixer on low speed, combine the flour, butter, and sugar until it forms grainy clumps; slowly stir in the egg yolks, vanilla sugar, nuts, and chocolate. Wrap the dough tightly in plastic wrap and let it rest for ½–1 hour in the fridge.

Roll out the dough on a floured surface until it is ½ inch thick. Transfer the dough to a baking sheet lined with parchment paper. Roll out the dough so that it covers nearly the entire surface of the pan. Bake for 15–20 minutes. Remove and cut into rectangular pieces, about 1½ x ½ inches.

CHOCOLATE TERRINE ON A PRALINE CRUST

Soft and creamy terrine of dark chocolate on a crispy nut crust. . .
Great with dark berries like blueberries, cherries and blackberries.

12 PORTIONS

Crust

¾ cup hazelnuts

2 tbsp granulated sugar

1 tbsp brown sugar

2 large eggs

1 tbsp all-purpose flour

Filling

12 oz dark chocolate (64–70%)

1 tbsp corn syrup or glucose

2 large eggs

⅓ cup milk

2 tbsp strong coffee, such as
espresso

2 tbsp heavy cream

Preheat the oven to 350°F. Toast the nuts in a dry frying pan over medium heat until light golden. Sprinkle the sugar and brown sugar over the nuts and swirl the pan as it melts. Continue cooking, without stirring, until the sugar turns a golden caramel color. Pour the mixture out onto a piece of parchment paper. Let cool and then break it up into very small pieces in a bowl. Add the eggs and flour to the praline (caramelized nuts) and stir until combined. Pour the mixture into a terrine mold or loaf pan lined with parchment paper. Bake in the center of the oven for about 10 minutes. Remove the pan from the oven and reduce the oven temperature to 200°F.

Chop the chocolate and melt it over a water bath. Whisk the syrup and eggs in a large bowl until the mixture is foamy. Bring the milk, coffee, and cream to a boil. Fold the melted chocolate into the whipped eggs and then, while whisking, gradually pour in the warm milk mixture until combined. Pour the batter into the pan over the crust and bake in the center of the oven for 35–40 minutes.

Remove the terrine, let cool to room temperature, and chill until firm enough to slice.

CHESTNUT TERRINE

The chestnut in this terrine is soft and creamy with an unusual, earthy flavor when paired with the chocolate.

12 PORTIONS

10½ oz dark chocolate
  (64–70%)

300 g (about 2 sticks plus
  5 tbsp) butter, divided

15½ oz unsweetened chestnut
  puree (1 can)

10½ oz white chocolate

Caramel Sauce

1 tbsp honey

3½ oz granulated sugar

½ cup heavy cream

50 g (about 3½ tbsp) butter

Chop the dark chocolate and let it melt together with 150 g (about 1¼ stick) of the butter over a water bath or in the microwave. Stir occasionally. Add half of the chestnut puree and beat with an electric mixer until smooth. Line a 1½-quart terrine mold or loaf pan with plastic wrap and pour in half of the dark chocolate mixture. Place the pan in the fridge for 1 hour.

Chop the white chocolate and carefully melt it together with the remaining butter over a water bath or in the microwave. Stir in the remaining chestnut puree. Pour half of the mixture over the chocolate in the pan and let it stand in the fridge for another hour.

Layer the separate chocolate mixtures one more time, letting each layer stand in the fridge for an hour. After the final layer has been in the fridge for an hour, chill for an additional 3–4 hours in the fridge. To serve, use the plastic wrap to lift the terrine out of the pan and use a sharp knife to cut into thick slices.

Melt the honey in a pot over medium heat. Add in the sugar a little at a time and cook until the mixture turns a light caramel color. Carefully add the cream, remove from heat, and stir in the butter. Let it cool briefly before drizzling over slices of the terrine.

CHOCOLATE CRUMBLE

Creamy chocolate filling and crispy, crumble topping . . . this pie goes well with liqueurs, Madeira, or port wine.

ABOUT 10 PORTIONS

Pie Shell

1¼ cups all-purpose flour

1 tsp baking powder

125 g (about 1 stick plus
    1 tbsp) butter

¾ cup powdered sugar

1 large egg yolk

1 tbsp cold water

Filling

7 oz dark chocolate

⅔ cup heavy cream

⅔ cup milk

2 large eggs

Crumble

⅔ cup packed light brown
    sugar

⅔ cup pecans, chopped

3½ oz dark chocolate
    (64–70%), chopped

3 oz sugar cookies or graham
    crackers (8–10 cookies),
    crumbled

60 g (about 4 tbsp) room
    temperature butter

1 tsp cacao powder

In a food processor, pulse the flour, baking powder, butter, and powdered sugar together until they begin to clump together. Add the egg yolk and water and pulse until the dough comes together. Wrap tightly in plastic wrap and chill for 30 minutes. Preheat the oven to 400°F. Roll the dough out on a floured surface and line a 9-inch pie plate with it; trim the edges. Prick holes in the bottom with a fork and bake the pie shell for 10–12 minutes, until set. Remove the crust from the oven.

Lower the oven temperature to 350°F. Chop the chocolate and place it in a bowl. Bring the cream and milk to a boil and pour it over the chocolate; stir until all the chocolate has melted. Whisk the eggs and mix into the chocolate. Fill the pie shell with the filling and bake for 18–20 minutes. Let the filling cool.

In a bowl, combine the ingredients for the crumble until it holds together in clumps. Sprinkle the crumble over the pie and place in the oven. Bake for about 15 minutes. Remove the pie and let cool. Refrigerate for a few hours before serving so that the filling firms up.

MINI CHOCOLATE PIES

These pies are really good and simple to make, even if it takes a little time to boil the dulce de leche filling.

8 PORTIONS

Filling

1 can of sweetened
   condensed milk

Crust

100 g (about 7 tbsp) cold
   butter
½ cup granulated sugar
1¼ cups all-purpose flour
¼ cup cacao powder
1 large egg

Icing

3½ oz dark chocolate
   (56–70%)
¼ cup heavy cream
2 tsp butter
Optional pinch sea salt

Place the unopened can of condensed milk into a pot and cover completely with water. Bring to a boil, then reduce the heat to a simmer and cook for about 4 hours. Add water to the pot now and then so that the water doesn't boil off completely. This caramelizes the sugar in the milk and creates a caramel-like, creamy filling (dulce de leche). Let the can cool at least 30 minutes before opening.

In a food processor, pulse the butter, sugar, flour, and cacao together until they begin to clump together. Add the egg and pulse until the dough holds together. Wrap the dough tightly in plastic wrap and set in the fridge for an hour.

Roll out the dough and line 8 mini pie pans, 2–3 inches in diameter, with the dough. Prick the dough with a fork and freeze the pie shells for 1 hour. Preheat the oven to 350°F and bake the shells directly from the freezer, for 7–8 minutes. To prevent the pie shells from bubbling, line each tin with parchment paper and fill them with dried beans or lentils while the shells bake. Remove the parchment and beans and let the pie shells cool. Fill the pie shells with the cooled dulce de leche.

Chop the chocolate and melt it. Add the cream and butter and stir gently on low heat until smooth and glossy. Add sea salt, if using. Pour over the pies and let stand until set.

DARK TRUFFLE BISKVIER

Chocolate biskvier is a classic cookie filled with buttercream. The more luxurious version has a chocolate truffle filling and is named after French actress Sarah Bernhardt.

20 BISKVIER

Bottom

9 oz almond paste

⅔ cup granulated sugar

2 large egg whites

Filling

4½ tbsp granulated sugar

¼ cup water

3 large egg yolks

150 g (about 1¼ stick) room
   temperature butter

2½ oz dark chocolate
   (64–70%)

Dipping

3½ oz dark chocolate
   (64–70%)

1 tbsp coconut butter

Preheat the oven to 350°F. Put the almond paste into a standing mixer and mix briefly to break it up. Add the sugar and egg whites and mix until well incorporated and smooth. Pipe or spoon out 20 even rounds on a baking sheet lined with parchment paper. Bake the bottoms in the center of the oven for 12–13 minutes. Remove the pan and let the cookies cool.

Boil the sugar and water together until they become viscous and thickened; remove from the heat. Whisk the egg yolks, and while whisking, pour them into the sugar mixture in a thin stream. Whisk vigorously until the mixture has cooled. Whisk the butter in a separate bowl and stir in the egg mixture a little at a time. Melt the chocolate and let it come to room temperature. Whisk the chocolate in a thin stream into the batter. Turn the cookie bottoms upside down and pipe the filling onto the cookies (or spread it on with an offset spatula). Place the cookies in the fridge.

Melt the chocolate and coconut butter in a pot over low heat; stir until it is smooth. Transfer it to a bowl and let cool until room temperature. Dip the tops of the cookies in the chocolate and return them upright to the pan to set.

SOUFFLÉ WITH WHISKEY ICE CREAM

Fluffy chocolate soufflé with raw sugar and cacao.

4 PORTIONS

2½ oz dark chocolate
   (70–75%)
2 tsp cacao
2 tbsp raw sugar
Butter for the ramekins
1 cup milk
25 g (about 2 tbsp) butter
2 tbsp all-purpose flour
2 large eggs, separated
2 tbsp whiskey
Cacao powder, for dusting

½ vanilla bean
⅔ cup heavy cream
¾ cup milk
3 large egg yolks
½ cup raw sugar
2 tbsp whiskey

Preheat the oven to 400°F. Chop the chocolate and set aside. Combine the cacao powder and raw sugar. Butter and "flour" four soufflé ramekins with a little butter together with the cacao sugar. Melt the chocolate in milk in a pot over low heat; whisk until completely dissolved and transfer it to a bowl. Melt the butter and whisk it into the chocolate milk. Whisk the flour into the chocolate milk and stir in the egg yolks once the batter is lukewarm. Whip the egg whites until foamy, white peaks form (do not overbeat). Stir the whiskey into the chocolate batter and then fold in the egg whites. Divide the batter between the ramekins and bake in the center of the oven for 15–20 minutes. Dust with cacao.

WHISKEY ICE CREAM

Slice the vanilla bean, scrape the seeds, and put them, along with the bean, into a saucepan with the cream and milk; bring to a boil over medium heat. Whisk the egg yolks and raw sugar together in a bowl until fluffy. Pluck out the vanilla bean and while whisking, pour the warm cream and milk over the eggs in an even stream. Pour the mixture back into the pot and heat gently while vigorously whisking until it reaches 185°F and begins to thicken. Don't let it boil.

Remove from the heat. Pour the mixture into a bowl and let cool. For best results, chill the base in the fridge overnight to deepen the flavor. Strain and add the whiskey. Run through an ice cream machine according to the manufacturer's instructions and freeze at least 1–2 hours.

CHOCOLATE DANISH

Rolled dough requires a little extra time and patience. Think "slow food"!

ABOUT 30 PIECES

1 cup cold water

1¾ oz fresh yeast

2 large eggs

2 tbsp granulated sugar

½ tsp salt

50 g (about 3½ tbsp) cold
   butter, sliced into cubes

4–4½ cups (1⅓ lbs)
   all-purpose flour

300 g (about 2 sticks plus
   5 tbsp) butter for rolling

1 large egg white for brushing

2½ oz dark chocolate
   (64–70%)

Pour the water into a standing mixer fitted with the dough hook. Add the yeast, eggs, sugar, salt, butter, and flour, a little at a time. Mix until a smooth dough forms; wrap it tightly in plastic wrap and chill it in the fridge for about 30 minutes. While the dough chills, make the vanilla cream (see the next page).

Roll out the dough on a lightly floured surface into a square, about 14 x 14 inches. On a piece of parchment, flatten the butter with a rolling pin until it becomes just about half the size of the dough. Place the butter on half of the dough on one side and fold the other half of the dough over the butter. Tap lightly with the rolling pin and roll the dough out to the original width. Fold the side edges toward the middle so that they meet in the center; carefully roll out again. Do this two more times (threefold). Rotate the dough a half turn after each time and flour lightly. If the dough gets too soft during this process, chill it briefly before rolling again.

Preheat the oven to 475°F. Let the dough rest for 15 minutes in the fridge under a dish towel. Then place it on a cutting surface and slice into ¾-inch-wide strips. Twist the strips lightly and place them in round coils on a baking sheet lined with parchment paper. Let rise for 15 minutes. Next, brush with egg white and place a dollop of vanilla cream in the center. Bake in the center of the oven for 7 minutes. Remove the Danish and let them cool

on the paper. Then transfer the pastries onto a rack so that they don't become soggy underneath.

Chop the chocolate, melt in the microwave, and drizzle over the pastries.

VANILLA CREAM

½ cup heavy cream

½ cup milk

2 tbsp cornstarch

2 tbsp granulated sugar

½ vanilla bean or 1½ tbsp
   vanilla sugar

2 egg yolks

Slice the vanilla bean and scrape out the seeds. Combine all the ingredients in a heavy-bottomed saucepan. While whisking constantly, heat the mixture over medium-low heat until the mixture is very thick. Remove the vanilla bean. Quickly transfer the cream into a cold bowl so that it doesn't get too warm. Cool to room temperature before storing in the refrigerator until ready to use.

CHOCOLATE SALAMI

Enjoy with a cup of coffee or as an accompaniment to dessert. It's exciting to combine this salami-like chocolate roll with dessert cheeses like brie or goat cheese together with a little blueberry marmalade.

1 ROLL, 20–25 PIECES

10½ oz dried figs

2 tbsp cognac

1½ oz shelled pistachios

1½ oz walnut halves

1½ oz almonds

2½ oz dates (pitted)

1¾ oz dark chocolate (70%)

1 pinch ground cinnamon

1 pinch ground clove

Rinse the figs and cut off the hard stems. Finely chop them and place in a bowl. Pour the cognac over them and let them soak for 30 minutes. Pulse the figs in a food processor until a thick paste forms and transfer it to a bowl. Coarsely chop the nuts, dates, and chocolate and add them to the bowl with the fig paste, along with the spices. Stir the fig mixture with a wooden spoon until very well combined. Form the mixture into a log, about 1½ inches wide, and wrap it tightly in waxed paper or parchment paper.

Let the roll stand in a cool place for at least 24 hours. Cut the salami into ¼-inch slices with a serrated knife.

LICORICE & CHOCOLATE

Licorice and chocolate work amazingly well together in the right proportions. It works best when the chocolate contains 45–65% cacao; if the content rises above 70% then the flavors clash with one another. In my recipes I use raw licorice in powdered form (granulated licorice) made from licorice root.

LICORICE CROQUANT

Crispy croquant flavored with licorice and dipped in chocolate.

30 PIECES

50 g (about 3½ tbsp) butter

⅔ cup granulated sugar

¼ cup light corn syrup or
   glucose

1 tsp granulated licorice (raw
   licorice powder)

5 drops salted licorice
   flavoring or 1 tsp salted
   licorice powder

Optional black food coloring

¼ cup walnut halves

¼ cup salted peanuts

7 oz dark chocolate (56–68%)
   or milk chocolate

Put the butter, sugar, syrup, powdered licorice and licorice flavoring into a heavy-bottomed stainless steel saucepan. Melt together, stirring, over low heat. Bring the mixture to a boil and cook to soft-crack stage, about 288°F. (To test with the ball method, see page 22.)

Spread out the mixture on a baking sheet lined with parchment paper. Cut the mixture into squares before it hardens.

Finely chop the nuts and set aside. Chop the chocolate and temper it (see page 20). Dip the croquant pieces in the chocolate with a dipping fork. Scrape off the croquant bottoms against the edge of the bowl and place the pieces on a piece of parchment paper.

Sprinkle the chopped nuts over the surface before the chocolate hardens.

LICORICE CARAMELS WITH CHOCOLATE & BLACK SALT

You can find black "lava salt" in specialty spice shops and food markets.
You can use ordinary flaked sea salt if you can't find black salt.

30-40 PIECES

1½ oz dark chocolate
   (64–70%)

¾ cup granulated sugar

¾ cup heavy cream

½ tbsp raw licorice powder

1¾ oz corn syrup or honey or
   glucose

Vegetable oil for the pan

Optional black food coloring

Dipping

9 oz dark chocolate (64–70%)

1 tsp black salt, lava salt, or
   flaked salt

Chop the chocolate and set aside. Boil the sugar, cream, and licorice on low heat until the sugar completely dissolves. Add the corn syrup or honey and chocolate. Boil until it reaches 250–255°F. Pour the caramel mixture in an oiled metal pan, about 6 x 8 inches, or in a pan lined with parchment paper. Let the caramel cool in the pan and stand at room temperature overnight.

Chop the chocolate for dipping and temper it (see page 20). Dip the caramels in the chocolate with a dipping fork and place them on parchment paper. Sprinkle pinches of salt over every caramel before the chocolate has time to harden.

To get a black caramel color, add a few drops of black food coloring to the caramel mixture.

LICORICE SHARDS

There are all sorts of licorice powders and all work well with these shards. You should still be mindful not to use chocolate with cacao content greater than 70% so the flavors don't clash.

3-4 SHEETS

10½ oz chocolate (54–65%)

3 tsp licorice powder or
    ground licorice root

Chop the chocolate and temper it (see page 20). Thinly spread the chocolate on heavy plastic wrap or overhead transparency film (acetate), and sprinkle licorice powder evenly over the surface. Let harden at room temperature or stand for a few minutes in the fridge. Remove the plastic and break the chocolate into shards. Serve as a candy or use as a garnish on ice cream, mousse, cakes, and desserts.

SALTED-LICORICE PRALINES

In order to create this beautiful pattern, drizzle black food coloring in the praline forms before filling with tempered chocolate.

ABOUT 30 PIECES

3½ oz dark chocolate
   (64–70%)

3½ oz milk chocolate

3 tbsp plus 1 tsp heavy cream

2 tbsp honey

2 tsp salted-licorice powder

25 g (about 2 tbsp) butter

Praline Shell

About 14 oz dark chocolate
   (56–64%)

Chop the dark and the milk chocolate and place in a bowl. Bring the cream, honey, and salted-licorice powder to a boil in a saucepan; pour the warm cream mixture over the chocolate and stir until all the chocolate has melted. If needed, place in the microwave for a few seconds. Stir in the butter and blend with a hand mixer.

Fill a disposable piping bag with the truffle filling.

Mold the praline shell (see page 24). Pipe in the filling and seal the pralines.

SEA BREEZE BARS

White chocolate is not as dominant as dark chocolate, and this combination brings out the delicate, licorice flavor.

3 BARS (EACH 3½ OZ)

10½ oz white chocolate

2 tsp raw licorice powder

½–1 tsp flaked sea salt

Chop the chocolate and temper it (see page 20). Stir half of the licorice powder into the chocolate. Sprinkle a little powder into the molds. Pour the chocolate into the molds and tap them lightly on the table to remove any air bubbles. Let the chocolate rest several minutes in the molds.

Sprinkle more licorice powder and flaked salt over the surface of the bars before the chocolate is completely set. Let the bars stand at room temperature overnight or in the fridge for 10–20 minutes. Turn the molds upside down and carefully tap out the chocolate.

Store in a cool place, 60–65°F.

PRALINES & TRUFFLES

AZTEC PRALINES

Really dark praline shells go well with these pralines dominated by spicy South American flavors.

ABOUT 30 PIECES

4½ oz dark chocolate
   (68–70%)
3½ oz milk chocolate
½ vanilla bean
6 tbsp plus 2 tsp heavy cream
2 tbsp dark honey
10 coffee beans
½ cinnamon stick
1 small piece of dried chili,
   such as ancho or árbol
1 tbsp dark rum or tequila
1 tbsp room temperature
   butter

Praline Shell

About 14 oz dark chocolate
   (64–70%)

Chop the dark chocolate and the milk chocolate and place in a bowl.

Split the vanilla bean lengthwise, scrape out the seeds and put them in a saucepan with the cream, honey, coffee beans, and spices, and bring to a boil.

Pour the warm cream mixture through a fine strainer over the chocolate and stir until all the chocolate has melted. Stir in the rum and butter and use a hand mixer to mix into a smooth filling. Fill a disposable piping bag with the mixture and let cool.

Mold the praline shells (see page 24). Pipe in the filling and seal the shells.

TIP!! Let the spices soak in the cream for a few hours before boiling it in order to intensify the flavor.

LEMON PRALINES

Shells of dark or milk chocolate really complement this sour praline filling balanced with coconut cream.

ABOUT 25 PIECES

7 oz white chocolate

¼ cup coconut cream

½ tbsp light honey, such
   as acacia

½ lemon, finely grated
   zest and 1–2 tsp juice

Praline Shell

About 14 oz dark chocolate
   (64–70%) or milk chocolate

Chop the chocolate, place in a bowl, and melt the chocolate in short intervals in a microwave. Bring the coconut cream and honey to a boil in a pan and pour it in the chocolate. Stir until everything is blended. Add the lemon zest and juice. Fill a disposable piping bag with the filling.

Mold the praline shells (see page 24). Pipe in the filling and seal the pralines.

DULCE DE LECHE TRUFFLES

Dulce de leche is the name of this wonderful caramel cream made with condensed milk boiled in its can for several hours.

ABOUT 25 PIECES

3½ oz dark chocolate
   (64–70%)

3 tbsp plus 1 tsp heavy cream

¼ cup dulce de leche (see
   page 127 for instructions),
   warmed

Optional licorice powder

Praline Shell

About 14 oz dark chocolate
   (56–70%)

Chop the chocolate, place in a bowl, and melt in the microwave. Bring the cream to a boil and pour over the chocolate. Stir in the warm dulce de leche. Fill a disposable piping bag with the mixture.

Mold the praline shells (see page 24) and pipe in the filling. Seal the pralines.

If you want dulce de leche filling with a licorice flavor, you can add 1 tsp of powdered licorice to the heavy cream after it is heated and before pouring it over the chocolate.

FIG TRUFFLES

Small truffles that pair well with coffee and aperitifs. Try with homemade coffee liqueur (see page 237).

ABOUT 60 PIECES

7 oz dark chocolate (70%)

2 fresh ripe figs

¼ cup water

¼ cup raw sugar

½ cup heavy cream

1 tsp room temperature butter

1 tsp whiskey

½ cup cacao powder

Chop the chocolate and place in a bowl. Rinse the figs, clip off the hard stems, and cut into pieces. Boil the fig pieces in the water and raw sugar for about 3 minutes. Strain off the syrup and mash the figs in the bottom of a bowl. Place the fig mash back in the pot and combine with the cream and butter. Bring that to a boil, then pour it over the chocolate and stir until all the chocolate has melted. Add the whiskey. Pour the mixture in a plastic wrap–lined pan, about 5 x 8 inches. Let stand in the fridge overnight.

Cut the truffle into pieces, about ¼-inch square, and roll the pieces in sifted cacao. Store in a cool place in a container with an airtight lid.

HAZELNUT PRALINES

Crispy and light bites with a classic hazelnut praliné. Read more about praliné on page 249.

ABOUT 45 PIECES

Praliné

2½ oz chopped hazelnuts

¼ cup granulated sugar

1 tbsp water

5 oz milk chocolate

1¾ oz dark chocolate
   (64–70%)

¾ cup heavy cream

Praline Shell

About 1 lb milk chocolate

Toast the hazelnuts in a dry frying pan, pour them out onto a dish towel, and rub off the thin skins. Melt the sugar and water in a skillet over medium heat and cook, swirling the pan until it turns a light caramel color. Fold the hazelnuts into the mixture and pour all of it out onto parchment paper. Let cool.

Chop the nut mixture coarsely and place in a food processor and pulse until finely chopped. Chop the chocolate and place it in a bowl. Bring the cream to a boil and pour it over the chocolate. Stir until all the chocolate has melted.

Let the chocolate cool to room temperature. Fold in the hazelnut praliné and fill a disposable piping bag with the filling.

Mold the praline shells (see page 24). Pipe in the filling and seal the pralines.

NIBS & CACAO PRALINES

Molding pralines with cacao powder can be a little tricky—but they'll definitely be beautiful!

ABOUT 35 PIECES

3½ oz dark chocolate
   (64–70%)
4 oz milk chocolate
3 tbsp plus 1 tsp heavy cream
1¾ oz honey
15 g (about 1 tbsp) butter
1 tbsp dark rum
1–2 tsp cacao powder
1–2 tsp cacao nibs

Praline Shells

About 14 oz dark chocolate
   (64–70%)

Chop the chocolate and place in a bowl. Bring the cream and honey to a boil, pour it over the chocolate, and stir until all the chocolate has melted. Stir the butter and rum into the chocolate. Mix the chocolate filling until smooth with a hand mixer.

Fill a disposable piping bag with the chocolate filling (ganache). Dust the praline forms lightly with cacao and sprinkle a few nibs in every praline mold.

Mold the praline shells (see page 24). Pipe in the filling and seal the pralines.

SINGLE ESTATE ECUADOR PRALINES

Pure chocolate from Ecuador has a deep and distinct cacao flavor without bitterness.

ABOUT 40 PIECES

7 oz dark chocolate from
    Ecuador (70%)

½ vanilla bean

⅓ cup cream

2 tbsp dark honey

1½ tbsp tequila

25 g (about 2 tbsp) room
    temperature butter

Praline Shell

About 1 lb dark chocolate
    from Ecuador (70%)

Chop the chocolate and place in a bowl. Split the vanilla bean lengthwise, scrape out the seeds, and put them in a saucepan with the cream and honey, and bring the mixture to a boil. Pour the warm cream mixture over the chocolate and stir until all the chocolate has melted. Remove the vanilla bean.

Stir the tequila and butter into the chocolate and mix into a smooth filling using a hand mixer. Fill a disposable piping bag with the filling and let cool.

Mold the praline shells (see page 24). Pipe in the filling and seal the pralines.

BLACK CURRANT PRALINES

Black currants have a natural acidity and go well with chocolate. These pralines, like all berry pralines, will not keep as long as other pralines because the berry filling contains more liquid.

ABOUT 30 PIECES

7 oz milk chocolate

6 tbsp plus 2 tsp heavy cream

1 tbsp light honey, such as
   acacia

¼ cup black currant puree
   (blended and strained
   berries)

Praline Shell

About 14 oz dark chocolate
   (56–64%)

Chop the chocolate and place in a bowl. Bring the cream, honey, and black currant puree to a boil. Pour the cream mixture over the chocolate and stir until everything has melted. Fill a disposable piping bag with chocolate filling and let cool.

Mold the praline shells (see page 24). Pipe in the filling and seal the pralines.

It also works well to replace the black currant puree with other berry purees, for example, raspberry, blackberry, or blueberry.

TRUFFLES

6 oz dark chocolate (64–70%)

6 tbsp plus 2 tsp heavy cream

Dipping

5 oz dark chocolate (55–64%)
or cacao powder and
powdered sugar

DARK TRUFFLES

Chop the chocolate and place in a bowl. Bring the cream to a boil and pour over the chocolate. Stir until all the chocolate has melted or alternatively melt in a microwave for a few seconds. Fill a disposable piping bag with the mixture and let cool at a cool room temperature overnight.

Pipe the truffle into lengths, about ¾–1¼ inches, or form into balls. Dip in tempered chocolate or sifted cacao powder and powdered sugar (combine 80% cacao powder and 20% powdered sugar).

ABOUT 20 PIECES

7 oz milk chocolate

3 tbsp plus 1 tsp heavy cream

1 tbsp glucose or 2 tsp honey

Dipping

5 oz dark chocolate (55–64%)
or cacao powder and
powdered sugar

MILK CHOCOLATE TRUFFLES

Chop the chocolate and place in a bowl. Bring the cream and glucose or honey to a boil and pour it over the chocolate. Stir until all the chocolate has melted or alternatively melt in a microwave for a few seconds. Fill a disposable piping bag with the mixture and let cool at a cool room temperature overnight.

Pipe the truffle mixture into lengths, about ¾–1¼ inches, or form into balls. Dip in tempered chocolate or sifted cacao powdered and powdered sugar (combine 80% cacao powder and 20% powdered sugar).

7 oz white chocolate

3 tbsp plus 1 tsp heavy cream

1 tbsp glucose or 2 tsp honey

2 tsp coffee liqueur

Dipping

5 oz dark chocolate (55-64%)
   or cacao powder and
   powdered sugar

ABOUT 30 PIECES

5 oz milk chocolate

2½ oz dark chocolate (70%)

2 tbsp honey, such as
   forest honey

1/3 cup heavy cream

25 g (about 2 tbsp) butter

1 tsp vodka

Dipping

5 oz dark chocolate (55-64%)
   or cacao powder and
   powdered sugar

WHITE TRUFFLES

Chop the chocolate and place in a bowl. Bring the cream and glucose or honey to a boil and pour it over the chocolate. Stir until all the chocolate has melted or alternatively melt in a microwave for a few seconds. Add the coffee liqueur. Fill a disposable piping bag with the mixture and let cool at room temperature overnight.

Pipe the truffle into lengths, about ¾-1¼ inches, or form into balls. Dip in tempered chocolate or sifted cacao powder and powdered sugar (combine 80% cacao powder and 20% powdered sugar).

HONEY TRUFFLES

Chop the chocolate and place in a bowl. Pour the honey in a pot and boil to about 250°F until the honey is caramelized. Carefully pour in the cream and bring it to a boil. Remove from heat and pour it over the chocolate. Mix with a hand mixer and stir in the butter and vodka.

Pour the truffle into a pan, about 4 x 7 inches, and cut into pieces. Dip in tempered chocolate or toss in sifted cacao powder and powdered sugar (combine 80% cacao powder and 20% powdered sugar).

ICE CREAM & CHOCOLATE

BROWNIE ICE CREAM

Serve this ice cream either with pieces of brownie or all by itself as a pure chocolate ice cream.

6–8 SERVINGS

½ vanilla bean

1¼ cups heavy cream

1¼ cups milk

2 tbsp honey

4 oz dark chocolate (56–65%)

5 large egg yolks

½ cup granulated sugar

2 brownies (see page 90)

Split the vanilla bean lengthwise, scrape out the seeds, and put them in a saucepan along with the cream, milk, and honey, and bring it to a boil. Remove from heat.

Chop the chocolate and place in a bowl. Whisk the yolks and sugar until fluffy. Remove the vanilla bean from the pot. While whisking, slowly pour the warm cream mixture into the whipped eggs, and then pour everything back into the pot. Heat, stirring constantly, until the temperature reaches 185°F or until it begins to thicken. Remove from heat, pour the hot cream over the chopped chocolate, and stir until very smooth.

Strain the mixture through a fine mesh sieve into a clean bowl; let it cool. Set the bowl in the fridge, preferably overnight, so that it becomes extra creamy.

Run the mixture through an ice cream machine according to the manufacturer's instructions until it is firm and creamy and then transfer it to a cake pan. Cut the brownie into pieces; mix the larger chunks into the ice cream and sprinkle the crumbs over the surface. Place in the freezer for at least an hour.

You might serve the ice cream with fresh raspberries or blackberries and lightly whipped cream.

MILK CHOCOLATE & BANANA POPSICLES

Making your own Popsicles is both simple and fun, and these days there is a wide variety of practical and whimsical ice cream molds.

ABOUT 6 POPSICLES

⅔ cup whipping cream

¾ cup milk

3 large egg yolks

¼ cup granulated sugar

2½ oz milk chocolate

1 small ripe banana

Ice cream molds

Popsicle sticks

Dipping

½ cup hazelnuts

3½ oz dark chocolate
   (56–64%)

Bring the cream and milk to a boil in a stainless steel pot. Whisk the egg yolks and sugar together in a bowl until light and foamy. While whisking, pour the warm cream into the eggs in a slow, thin stream. Pour the mixture back into the saucepan and place back on the stove. Warm gently while vigorously whisking until it reaches 185°F or until it begins to thicken.

Pour the mixture in a bowl. Chop the milk chocolate and stir into the warm cream mixture. Stir until all the chocolate has melted. Puree the banana using a hand mixer and then stir it into the ice cream mixture. Let cool. Run the mixture through an ice cream machine according to manufacturer's instructions, and then fill a disposable piping bag with the ice cream. Fill the chambers of a 6-portion Popsicle mold. Place in the freezer for a few hours. Remove and insert the Popsicle sticks just as the ice cream has begun to harden. Let stand in the freezer overnight so that the Popsicles loosen a little from the molds.

Toast the hazelnuts in a dry frying pan. Pour them out onto a kitchen towel and rub off the thin skins. Chop the nuts into small bits and set aside.

Rinse the mold with lukewarm water to loosen the Popsicles. Place the unmolded Popsicles on a tray lined with wax paper. Place back in the freezer. Chop the dipping chocolate and melt. Remove the Popsicles and dip the tops first in the chocolate and then in the nuts.

CHOCOLATE PARFAIT IN A GLASS

Enjoy with a cup of espresso.

6 PORTIONS

¾ cup heavy cream

¼ cup powdered sugar

2 large egg yolks

1¾ oz dark chocolate
   (64–70%)

Milk Chocolate Crisp

¾ oz milk chocolate

7 tsp corn syrup or glucose

1 oz powdered sugar

Garnish

1–2 tsp shaved chocolate or
   cacao powder

Lightly whip the cream. Whisk the powdered sugar and eggs until lightened and fluffy. Chop the dark chocolate and melt carefully in the microwave. Stir the chocolate into the eggs and then quickly fold in the cream. Divide the batter into six heavy, freezer-safe glasses. Place the glasses on a small tray and place in the freezer for at least 3 hours.

Chop the milk chocolate. Stir the corn syrup or glucose and powdered sugar together in a saucepan and heat over medium heat until it reaches 310–320°F. Remove from heat.

Add the chocolate to the sugar mixture and stir quickly. Pour the mixture on a silicone baking mat or on a baking sheet lined with parchment paper. Place another silicone mat or another piece of parchment paper on top and quickly roll out the mixture with a rolling pin. Work fast; otherwise it will harden!

Let the crisp harden and then break into pieces. Add a piece of chocolate crisp to the parfait. Garnish the parfait with shaved chocolate or dust with cacao.

CHOCOLATE POPSICLES WITH COCONUT

Cooling Popsicles with a slightly more intense chocolate flavor.

ABOUT 6 POPSICLES

¾ cup milk

⅔ cup heavy cream

3 large egg yolks

¼ cup granulated sugar

2½ oz dark chocolate
(64–70%)

Ice cream molds

Popsicle sticks

Dipping

3½ oz dark chocolate
(56–70%)

½ cup flaked coconut or
chopped hazelnuts

Bring the milk and cream to a boil in a saucepan. Whisk the egg yolks and sugar until lightened and foamy. While whisking, pour the warm milk in a slow stream into the eggs. Pour the mixture back in the pot and stir over medium heat until it reaches 185°F, or until it thickens. Make sure that it doesn't burn. Pour the mixture through a fine mesh strainer into a bowl.

Chop the chocolate and stir into the warm cream. Stir until everything has melted, then allow to cool. Run through an ice cream machine according to manufacturer's instructions and pour the thickened ice cream into a disposable piping bag. Pipe into the Popsicle mold.

Let stand in the freezer for a couple of hours. Remove the ice cream just when it begins to harden and insert the Popsicle sticks. Let the completed Popsicles stand in the freezer overnight.

Rinse the molds quickly with lukewarm water, loosen the Popsicles, and set them on a tray lined with wax paper. Place back in the freezer. Chop the chocolate and melt. Remove the Popsicles from the freezer, and dip the tops in chocolate and then in coconut or hazelnuts.

CHOCOLATE SORBET WITH ORANGE

Serve the sorbet as usual or as Popsicles.

6-8 PORTIONS OR ABOUT 6 POPSICLES

1 sheet gelatin

2⅛ cups water

⅔ cacao powder

1 cup granulated sugar

¾ cup water

2 tbsp honey

Finely grated zest and juice
   of ½ orange

Optional Popsicle molds

Optional Popsicle sticks

Soak the gelatin in a bowl of cold water for 5–10 minutes. Bring the 2⅛ cups water and cacao powder to a boil in a saucepan and whisk until all the cacao has dissolved. In another saucepan, boil the sugar, ¾ cup water, and honey for a few minutes. Remove the pot from heat. Lift the gelatin out of the water and stir it into the warm sugar syrup until melted. Combine the cacao water, sugar syrup, and orange zest and juice. Let the syrup cool and run through an ice cream machine according to the manufacturer's instructions.

Place the sorbet in the freezer or fill Popsicle molds. Insert the Popsicle sticks and let the sorbet stand overnight in the freezer. Remove and quickly run a little lukewarm water over the Popsicle molds to loosen them.

TARTUFO WITH CHERRIES & LIQUEUR

Maraschino is a cherry liqueur made since the 1500s in Zadar, Croatia, from a recipe originally created by monks. It is also produced in Italy. It's the cherries and this unique liqueur that make this ice cream so special.

6-8 PORTIONS

Marinated Cherries

2 tbsp granulated sugar

2 tbsp water

2 tbsp Maraschino liqueur

5 oz pitted cherries

Chocolate Ice Cream

1¼ cups heavy cream

1¼ cups milk

2 tbsp cacao powder

2 tbsp honey

5 large egg yolks

¼ cup granulated sugar

¼ cup muscovado sugar

3½ oz dark chocolate (64–70%)

Garnish

5 oz dark chocolate (64–70%) for rolling the ice cream balls

Bring the sugar and water to a boil in a saucepan; remove from the heat and add the liqueur. Chop the cherries and place them in the syrup. Let the cherries marinate for about 2 hours.

During this time, make the ice cream. Bring the cream, milk, cacao powder, and honey to a boil in a saucepan. Remove the pot from heat. Whisk the egg yolks, sugar, and muscovado sugar together in a bowl until fluffy. While whisking, pour the warm cream into the eggs and mix until combined, and then pour everything back in the pan. While stirring, heat the mixture until it reaches 185°F or until it begins to thicken. Remove the pot from heat.

Immediately pour the mixture through a fine mesh strainer into a clean bowl. Chop the chocolate and stir it into the warm ice cream mixture until everything has melted. Let the ice cream mixture cool sufficiently. Run it through an ice cream machine according to the manufacturer's instructions.

Drain the cherries and fold them into the semi-firm ice cream. Transfer the ice cream to a bowl and freeze for 1-2 hours. Grate the chocolate. Scoop out balls of ice cream and roll them in the grated chocolate as if coating truffles. Place the ice cream balls in cupcake liners and keep in the freezer until ready to serve.

MOCHI

Mochi is the name of these fine Japanese bundles. The Japanese prefer to fill them with red bean paste, while people in New York and Los Angeles prefer mochi filled with ice cream.

ABOUT 10 PIECES

Ice Cream
1 batch of brownie ice cream (see page 170)

Dough
1 cup rice flour (glutinous rice flour)

¾ cup water

¼ cup granulated sugar

2 tsp vanilla sugar or vanilla seeds from ½ vanilla bean

2 tbsp cornstarch

2 tbsp toasted, unshelled sesame seeds

Garnish
Cacao powder

3½ oz melted dark chocolate (56–64%)

Fresh fruit, such as melon, pear, mango, or fresh berries, such as raspberries

Make a batch of ice cream. Line a tray with plastic wrap and quickly scoop out 10 small chocolate ice cream balls and place them on the tray. Keep in the freezer while making the dough.

Combine the rice flour and water in a glass bowl. Add the sugar and vanilla. Cover with plastic wrap and place in the microwave for 2 minutes. Stir. Cover again with the plastic wrap and heat in the microwave for another 30 seconds. Remove the plastic and let the dough cool.

Wrap a cutting board in plastic wrap and dust it with half of the cornstarch. Turn the dough out onto the cutting board and let it cool completely. Dust the dough with the remaining cornstarch and turn the dough a few times. Wrap the dough in the plastic wrap and set in the fridge for 30–60 minutes, or until it is easy to roll out.

Return the dough to the cutting board. Divide into 10 pieces and roll each one out into thin rounds (for a more precise circle, press with a round cookie or dough cutter). Sprinkle some sesame seeds on each round and roll them lightly with the pin to adhere them. Take out the ice cream balls from the freezer, place the balls on the dough rounds, and work the dough around them. Place the bundles with the seam down on a little tray and immediately place in the freezer.

Remove the bundles 5 minutes before eating. Dust with cacao powder. Serve with melted chocolate and fresh fruit such as melon, pear, mango, or fresh berries such as raspberries.

CHOCOLATE SWEETS

CHOCOLATE-DIPPED MARSHMALLOWS

Foamy sweets with classic flavors: coconut and chocolate.

ABOUT 60 PIECES, BITE-SIZE

6 sheets gelatin

1 cup granulated sugar

½ cup water

¾ tsp glucose

1 large egg white

1 tbsp powdered sugar

1 tbsp cornstarch

About 10½ oz dark chocolate (64–70%)

4 tbsp flaked coconut

Soak the gelatin in a bowl of cold water for 5–10 minutes. Boil the sugar, water, and glucose together until it reaches 266°F in a stainless steel pot. Meanwhile, in a standing mixer, whip the egg white until soft peaks form. With the mixer on medium, slowly pour the hot sugar in a slow stream over the egg white, and continue whisking for a few minutes. Place the bowl in a cold water bath and continue whisking until the temperature lowers to 104°F and the mixture is smooth.

Drain the gelatin sheets, squeezing out the excess water and melt it in a bowl in the microwave. Whisk the gelatin into the egg and sugar mixture and whisk for a few minutes. Fill a disposable piping bag with the mixture and let it firm up for about 10–15 minutes at room temperature. Meanwhile, sift the powdered sugar and cornstarch together. Line a tray with parchment paper and dust it with the cornstarch–powdered sugar mixture. Pipe the filling the length of the tray in strips about ¾ inch wide. Let the tray stand at a cool room temperature overnight.

Cut the strips into pieces 1½ inches long. Melt the chocolate and temper it (see page 20). Dip the pieces in the chocolate and sprinkle the flaked coconut over the chocolate.

Keep cool in an airtight container.

CHOCOLATE CARAMELS

¾ cup granulated sugar

¾ cup heavy cream

7 tsp corn syrup or glucose
   or honey

1½ oz dark chocolate
   (56–64%)

Dipping

9 oz dark chocolate (56–64%)

Garnish

Optional 1 tbsp crushed
   cacao nibs or 1 tsp flaked
   sea salt

CHOCOLATE-DIPPED CHOCOLATE CARAMELS

Boil the sugar and cream in a heavy-bottomed saucepan until the sugar dissolves. Add the corn syrup and chocolate. Boil, without stirring, until it passes a ball test (see page 22) or to 251–253°F.

Pour the caramel into a cake pan lined with parchment paper, about 5 x 7 inches. Let the caramel harden at room temperature overnight. Cut into pieces.

Temper the chocolate (see page 20) and dip the caramels in chocolate with a dipping fork. (The chocolate needs to be tempered to ensure that it will harden and have a glossy appearance.)

Place the caramels on parchment paper. If you like, sprinkle cacao nibs or flaked sea salt over the chocolate before it sets.

30-40 PIECES

½ cup heavy cream

5 tbsp honey

⅔ cup granulated sugar

7 oz dark chocolate (56–58%)

¼ cup pistachio nuts

CHOCOLATE CARAMELS WITH PISTACHIO NUTS

Bring the cream, honey, and sugar to a boil in a heavy-bottomed saucepan. Chop the chocolate and add it to the cream, stirring until all the chocolate has melted. Boil until it passes a ball test (see page 22) or until 251–253°F. Stir all the way to the bottom now and then. Toward the end of cooking turn down the heat to avoid burning.

Pour the caramel in a cake pan lined with parchment paper, about 5 x 7 inches. Chop the pistachios and sprinkle them over the caramel. Let the caramel harden at room temperature overnight. Cut into pieces.

CHOCOLATE & PEANUT CUPS

Small, delicious sweets that are a simple variation on classic American peanut butter cups.

10 PIECES

Liners

3½ oz dark chocolate
   (64–70%)

Filling

1 tbsp salted peanuts
3½ oz dark chocolate
   (64–70%)
25 g (about 2 tbsp) butter
1½ oz peanut butter
10 mini paper candy liners

Chop the chocolate and temper it (see page 20). Brush the inside of the liners with chocolate. Let cool.

Finely chop the peanuts and set aside. Chop the chocolate for the filling and melt on low heat together with the butter and peanut butter. Stir in the peanuts.

Fill a disposable piping bag with the mixture and let cool. Pipe the filling into the chocolate liners.

Keep the cups in their liners in an airtight container.

CHOCOLATE HALVA

These goodies come originally from the Middle East and are not only tasty but nutritious—sesame seeds contain plenty of minerals and nutrients.

ABOUT 20 PIECES

Butter for the pan
2⅛ cups sesame seeds
½ tsp cinnamon
1¼ cups raw sugar
½ cup honey
¼ cup water
4 tbsp cacao powder
1¾ oz dark chocolate
   (56–64%)
Optional 1¾ oz chopped
   pistachios

Butter a loaf pan. Toast the sesame seeds lightly in a frying pan until light golden. Add them to the bowl of an electric mixer. Mix them together with the cinnamon.

Boil the sugar, honey, and water for about 10 minutes. With the mixer running on low, pour the sugar syrup in a fine stream into the seeds. Add the cacao powder. Coarsely chop the dark chocolate and fold into the mixture; mix until the chocolate is completely melted and evenly distributed. Stir in the pistachios if using. Spread the mixture into the pan and let stand at room temperature for a few hours. Slice with a sharp knife.

FUDGE WITH PEANUTS & MARSHMALLOWS

Easy-to-make fudge with a rich filling that combines sweet and salty, soft and crunchy.

24–30 PIECES

3½ oz milk chocolate

3½ oz dark chocolate (64%)

1 tbsp butter

½ can sweetened condensed milk

1 tsp vanilla sugar

⅔ cup marshmallows (minis or large ones cut into small pieces)

½ cup salted peanuts

Chop the chocolate and melt it together with the butter and condensed milk over a water bath. Remove from the heat, cool briefly, and stir in the vanilla sugar.

Fold in the marshmallows and peanuts, avoiding stirring too much, which would melt them.

Spread the fudge in a cake pan lined with parchment paper and let it harden in the fridge for a few hours. Cut the fudge into pieces with a sharp knife.

MOLDED CHOCOLATE BARS

It's fun to make these delicious chocolate bars. Wrap them in attractive paper to turn them into really nice going-away presents!

3 BARS (EACH 3½ OZ)

Dried Fruit

Apples (not mealy)

Pineapple rings

Milk Chocolate
Apple Pie

10½ oz milk chocolate

2 tbsp cake crumbs

6 thin and dried apple rings

3 pinches ground cinnamon

White Chocolate with
Green Tea and Mint

10½ oz white chocolate with
   vanilla

1 tsp green tea powder

1 tbsp dried mint leaves

5 drops peppermint oil

Dark Chocolate
Piña Colada

10½ oz dark chocolate
   (64–70%)

1 tbsp flaked coconut

3 pineapple rings

There are different methods for drying fruit, either in an oven or at room temperature.

Drying in the oven: Preheat the oven to 125°F. Core and slice the apples in ⅛-inch-thick slices. It works well to dry them with or without the peel. Place the apple slices on a baking sheet and set in the oven. Let dry for 2–3 hours. Let the apple slices remain in the oven for an hour after turning off the heat (open the oven door now and then to let out the steam) and then place them in a warm room overnight.

Drying at room temperature: Core the apples and cut them into ⅛-inch-thick slices. It works well to dry them with or without the peel. Hang the rings on a string with about 1 inch between them. Twine works perfectly well and can be found in cooking stores. Hand the string over a radiator or some other warm and dry place and let hand there for 2–3 days.

You can even dry the pineapple in the oven; it just takes a little longer. Slice pineapple into rings to dry at home.

Temper the chocolate (see page 20) and mold in chocolate bar molds (see page 24). Sprinkle the ingredients over the chocolate before it sets.

RASPBERRY & PASSION FRUIT YUMMIES

Two different versions of chocolate-dipped marshmallow cookies with fruit and berry flavors in an exciting combination. These goodies require a certain amount of practice.

ABOUT 60 PIECES

6 leaves of gelatin

1 cup granulated sugar

½ cup water

1 tsp corn syrup or glucose

1 large egg white

2 tbsp raspberry puree

2 tbsp mango puree or
   passion fruit puree
   (available ready-made)

Wafer

20 vanilla wafer cookies,
   about 1½ inch wide

12–14 oz dark chocolate
   (56–70%)

Garnish

2 tbsp freeze-dried
   raspberries

2 passion fruits, seeded

Preheat the oven to 175°F. Scoop out the contents of the passion fruits and spread out on a parchment-lined baking sheet. Let dry in the oven for about 1½ hours. Stir now and then.

Soak the gelatin in a bowl of cold water for 5–10 minutes.

In a small saucepan, boil the sugar, water, and corn syrup or glucose until it reaches 266°F. Meanwhile, when the sugar syrup reaches 248°F, beat the egg white in a standing mixer until foamy and firm. With the mixer running, pour the warm syrup over the egg whites and continue to whisk for a few minutes. Continue whisking until the temperature lowers to 104°F and the mixture is smooth. If it doesn't cool, then it will be grainy.

Drain the gelatin, squeeze the excess water from it and melt it in a small pan. Whisk the gelatin into the egg whites. Divide the batter into two bowls and add the raspberry and either the mango or passion fruit puree to each bowl. Whisk each combination until the mixture has completely cooled. Fill disposable piping bags with the fillings and pipe a kiss of the marshmallow on the tops of the round cookies.

Chop the dark chocolate and temper it (see page 20). Dip the tops in the chocolate and sprinkle either freeze-dried raspberries or the dried passion fruit seeds over the top.

PISTOLE WITH SPICES

Small, spiced chocolate disks; popular sweets served when invited to tea.

30–40 PIECES

Disks

7 oz dark chocolate
 (64–70%)

Garnish

Freeze-dried raspberry

Fennel

Anise

Sea salt or Himalayan salt

Cacao nibs

Melt the chocolate and temper (see page 20). Line a tray with parchment paper. Fill a disposable piping bag with the chocolate and pipe out disks, 1–1½ inches in diameter, onto the paper. Top with whatever sounds best: freeze-dried raspberry, fennel, anise, salt, or cacao nibs.

CARAMEL MARSHMALLOWS WITH WALNUTS

These bites are almost their own little dessert and require a little practice. Toasted walnuts make them extra crispy and lend a fantastic nutty taste.

ABOUT 60 PIECES

Marshmallows

5 leaves gelatin

1 cup granulated sugar

½ cup water

2 tbsp corn syrup or glucose

½ vanilla bean, Bourbon Vanilla from Madagascar

1 egg white

1 tbsp powdered sugar

1 tbsp cornstarch

Fudge Caramel

100 g (about 7 tbsp) butter

¾ cup heavy cream

1¼ cups granulated sugar

5 tbsp light corn syrup or glucose

About 1½ cups chopped walnuts

About 14 oz milk chocolate

Garnish

Chopped walnuts

Soak the gelatin in a bowl of cold water for 5–10 minutes. Boil the sugar, water, and corn syrup or glucose until it reaches 266°F. Split the vanilla bean lengthwise, scrape out the seeds, and put them in a standing mixer with the egg white. When the sugar reaches 248°F, whip the egg whites until soft peaks form. While whipping, pour the sugar syrup over the egg whites and continue whisking until cooled to room temperature. Drain the gelatin, squeeze out the excess water, and melt it in a small pot. Whisk the gelatin into the meringue mixture until completely combined and cool.

Continue whisking until the marshmallow has cooled to 104°F and until the mixture is smooth. If it doesn't cool, then it will be grainy. Combine the powdered sugar and cornstarch and sift it into the bottom of two 5 x 7-inch aluminum pans. Spread the mixture evenly in the pans and let stand at room temperature overnight.

Melt the butter in a heavy-bottomed saucepan. Stir in the cream, sugar, and corn syrup. Cover and let boil until it reaches 250–251°F. Stir now and then. Let the caramel cool to room temperature. Pour the caramel over the marshmallows and sprinkle the nuts evenly over the surface (save some for garnishing).

Let the caramel harden at room temperature. Cut into pieces with a sharp knife. Chop the chocolate and temper it (see page 20). Dip the pieces in the chocolate with a dipping fork. Place them on parchment paper and garnish with walnuts before the chocolate hardens.

SMALL DESSERTS

CHOCOLATE CREAM DULCE DE LECHE

A dessert in two layers that you can top in different ways, for example, with chopped, salted nuts, nibs, chocolate, or fresh berries.

10 SMALL PORTIONS IN A GLASS

1 can sweetened condensed milk
5 oz dark chocolate (64–70%)
3½ oz milk chocolate
1¼ cups heavy cream
1 large egg yolk
1 tsp vanilla sugar
25 g (about 2 tbsp) room temperature butter
2 tbsp dark rum

Garnish

1 tsp cacao nibs or chopped chocolate (54–70%)
1 tbsp chopped salted and roasted hazelnuts
Fresh berries, such as raspberries, blackberries, or cherries

Boil the unopened can of condensed milk in a pot covered with water for 4 hours. Refill with water as necessary so that the water doesn't boil away.

Remove the can from the pan and cool sufficiently, at least 20–30 minutes. Open carefully; if the can is still too warm there may be pressure in the can. Place 1 tbsp of the caramel sauce (dulce de leche) in the bottoms of 10 small liqueur or port wine glasses.

Chop the dark and milk chocolate and place in a bowl. Bring the cream to a boil and pour it over the chocolate, stirring until all the chocolate has melted. Whisk in the egg yolk, vanilla sugar, butter, and rum.

Distribute the chocolate cream between the glasses. Garnish with nibs or chocolate, or perhaps salted, roasted nuts. Let the glasses stand in the fridge until the cream has hardened. This takes about 3 hours. Serve with fresh berries.

CHOCOLATE MOUSSE

ABOUT 8 SERVINGS

5 oz dark chocolate (64–70%)

2 tbsp heavy cream

2 large egg yolks

¼ cup granulated sugar

2 tbsp strong, cold coffee

1⅔ cups heavy cream

Cacao for dusting

Garnish

1 tbsp chopped chocolate

CHOCOLATE MOUSSE

Chop the chocolate and melt on low heat together with the 2 tbsp cream, stirring so that the chocolate and cream are blended.

Whisk the egg yolks and sugar together until fluffy. Pour in the coffee. Whip the remaining cream until soft peaks form. Combine one-quarter of the whipped cream with the chocolate. Blend the whipped eggs and chocolate, and then gently fold in the rest of the cream.

Fill glasses with the mousse and smooth the surface with a spatula. Dust with cacao powder and garnish with chopped chocolate.

ABOUT 8 SERVINGS

9 oz dark chocolate (64%)

6 large eggs, separated

Garnish

1 tbsp cacao nibs or coarsely
    chopped chocolate

DARK CHOCOLATE MOUSSE WITH CACAO BEANS

Coarsely chop the chocolate and melt in intervals on low power in the microwave. Stir now and then. Whisk the egg yolks in one bowl, and whip the egg whites until soft peaks form in another. Whisk the egg yolks into the chocolate and then quickly fold in the whipped egg whites.

Pipe the mousse into glasses, preferably with the help of a disposable piping bag. Smooth out the surfaces and garnish with cacao nibs.

CHOCOLATE CRÈME BRÛLÉE

ABOUT 8 SERVINGS

½ vanilla bean

1¼ cups heavy cream

¾ cup milk

½ cup granulated sugar

2½ oz dark chocolate (70%)

4 large egg yolks

Raw sugar for caramelizing

Split the vanilla bean lengthwise and scrape out the seeds. Place the vanilla bean and scraped seeds in a saucepan. Pour in the cream, milk, and sugar. Stir and let come to a boil.

Chop the chocolate and place in a bowl. Remove the vanilla bean and pour the warm milk and cream over the chocolate and stir until the chocolate has melted. Whisk the egg yolks and fold them into the chocolate mixture, stirring everything together. Cover the bowl with plastic wrap and set in the fridge. For best results, let the mixture stand and "mature" in the fridge overnight.

Preheat the oven to 225°F. Pour the mixture into ramekins and place in the oven, baking for about 40 minutes or until the custard sets but still wobbles in the center. (If you like, place some raspberries on the bottom of the ramekins before pouring in the mixture.) Alternatively, bake in a water bath in the oven at 250°F for about 35 minutes or until the custard is set. Remove from the oven, let cool, and chill in the fridge. Sprinkle and even layer of raw sugar over each custard and caramelize it with a kitchen torch. You can also place the ramekins on the highest rack in the oven under the broiler for a few minutes with the oven door ajar (don't forget to watch them carefully!). Serve with fresh raspberries, vanilla ice cream, or cream.

TIP!! The brûlée can be prepared a day in advance. Keep in the fridge, covered with plastic wrap. Caramelize the sugar just prior to serving.

CHOCOLATE CREAM WITH NUTS & DRIED FRUIT

Top these small desserts with your choice of dried fruits, berries, and nuts. The salt in the nuts adds an extra dimension!

4 SERVINGS

3½ oz milk chocolate

1¾ oz dark chocolate (64%)

⅔ cup sour cream

2 tbsp hazelnuts

1 dash of vegetable oil

2 pinches salt

½ tsp granulated sugar

2 dried figs

2 tbsp dried cranberries

1½ oz nougat

Chop all the chocolate and melt in a microwave or a water bath. Stir in the sour cream. Fill small glasses and place them in the fridge.

Toast the nuts in a dry frying pan until light golden. Pour the oil, salt, and sugar over the nuts and continue cooking, tossing the pan, until the sugar caramelizes. Pour the nuts out onto a piece of parchment paper and cool completely.

Chop the nuts, dried fruit, and nougat and sprinkle over the cream.

CHOCOLATE PUDDING WITH MARSHMALLOWS

Soft, creamy, and old-fashioned chocolate pudding is a favorite with both children and adults!

6 SERVINGS

1¼ cups milk

½ cup heavy cream

¼ cup granulated sugar

1 tsp vanilla sugar

¼ cup cacao powder

2 large egg yolks

1¾ oz dark chocolate (70%)

1 tbsp cornstarch

¼ cup cold coffee

½ cup mini marshmallows

Garnish

1 tsp–1 tbsp cacao powder
   or shaved dark chocolate
   (70%)

Whisk the milk, cream, sugar, vanilla sugar, cacao powder, and egg yolks together in a saucepan.

Chop the chocolate and set aside. Dissolve the cornstarch in the cold coffee in a bowl and then stir it into the liquid in the pan. Heat the liquid over medium heat, whisking vigorously, until the cream begins bubble and thicken. Remove the pot from heat and stir in the chocolate. Whisk intensively until all the chocolate has melted. Pour the chocolate pudding into small coffee cups or glasses. Let stand in the fridge until the pudding has cooled.

Serve with lightly whipped cream and marshmallows. Dust with cacao powder or garnish with shaved chocolate.

CHOCOLATE SPREAD WITH HONEY & CHILI

Wonderful for dipping cherries and strawberries in! It can also be served on crostini or toasts with a little flaked sea salt.

1 JAR (ABOUT ¾ CUP)

3½ oz dark chocolate (64–70%)

3½ oz dark honey, such as chestnut honey or forest honey, room temperature

5–6 drops toasted sesame seed oil

Optional red chili (Spanish pepper)

Chop the chocolate and melt it over a water bath or in the microwave. Stir in the honey and sesame seed oil. Serve the cream lukewarm or at room temperature.

If you prefer the chocolate a little spicier, you can finely chop half of a red chili—Spanish pepper—and mix it into the chocolate cream. Don't forget to remove the chili seeds first!

COFFEE MOUSSE WITH DARK GANACHE

This mousse isn't as fluffy as ordinary mousse, but it is creamier and insanely good!

6 SERVINGS

3½ oz dark chocolate
 (54–65%)
6 tbsp plus 2 tsp heavy cream
1 large egg yolk
2 tbsp coffee (espresso or
 strongly brewed coffee)
1½ tbsp room temperature
 butter.

Dark Ganache

1¾ oz dark chocolate (70%)
3 tbsp plus 1 tsp heavy cream

Caramel Mousse

¼ cup granulated sugar
1 tbsp water
2 large egg yolks
1 tbsp cornstarch
6 tbsp plus 2 tsp milk
2 tbsp heavy cream
1 tsp room temperature
 butter

Garnish

2 dark chocolate cookies, such
 as chocolate cookie slices
 (see page 85), crumbled

Finely chop the chocolate and place in a bowl. Bring the cream to a boil. Place the egg yolk in a different bowl. While whisking, pour the cream over the egg yolk; pour the liquid back into the pot and cook on medium heat, stirring, until it reaches 183°F and begins to thicken. Pour the warm cream through a fine mesh strainer over the chocolate. Add the coffee and butter and whisk until combined. Fill a disposable piping bag with the mousse and distribute between 6 glasses. Refrigerate until firm.

For the ganache, finely chop the chocolate and place it in a bowl. Bring the cream to a boil and pour it over the chocolate, stirring until everything is melted. Let cool. Glaze the coffee mousse with the ganache and refrigerate.

Pour the sugar in a frying pan. Add the water, bring to a boil, and cook until it turns a deep caramel color. Pour the caramel on a baking sheet lined with parchment. Let cool and harden. Break into pieces and pulse in a food processor until it becomes a fine powder. Whisk the egg yolks and cornstarch together in a bowl. Bring the milk and cream to a boil and while whisking, pour the milk and cream into the egg yolks. Pour the mixture back in the pan and whisk vigorously until the mixture thickens and begins to simmer. Remove the pan from the heat, stir in the butter and caramel dust and continue whisking over a cold water bath until cooled to room temperature. Fill a piping bag with the caramel mousse and pipe a dollop onto the mousse and ganache. Garnish with crushed chocolate cookie crumbs.

MINI CARAMEL & PEANUT PIES

Soft caramel, crisp crust, salted peanuts, and silky milk chocolate make these small pies absolute delicacies!

ABOUT 8 PIES

Crust

75 g (about 5 tbsp) butter

¼ cup powdered sugar

½ cup all-purpose flour

2 tbsp cacao powder

1 tbsp water

Filling

50 g (about 3½ tbsp) butter

6 tbsp plus 2 tsp heavy cream

⅔ cup granulated sugar

¼ cup light corn syrup or
glucose

1 tbsp cacao powder

½ cup salted peanuts

Milk Chocolate Ganache

4 oz milk chocolate

½ cup heavy cream

Garnish

Optional shaved milk
chocolate

In a food processor, pulse the butter, powdered sugar, flour, and cacao together until crumbly. Mix in the water and pulse until the dough comes together. Wrap the dough tightly in plastic wrap and place in the fridge for 1 hour. Preheat the oven to 400°F. Roll out the dough and then line 8 mini pie tins. Bake for 6–8 minutes. For best results, line the crusts with parchment paper, fill with dried yellow peas or beans, and then remove them after baking the piecrusts.

Melt the butter in a heavy-bottomed stainless steel saucepan. Stir in the cream, sugar, syrup, and cacao powder and boil until the temperature reaches 246–250°F. It's important not to let the caramel boil too long or get too hot; otherwise it will be too hard. Stir now and then.

Remove the pan from the heat and let the caramel cool a bit. Distribute the peanuts into all the piecrusts. Pour in the caramel and let it cool completely.

Chop the chocolate and place it in a bowl. Bring the cream to a boil and pour it over the chocolate. Stir until all the chocolate has melted. Pour the ganache over the caramel and let harden. If you like, garnish with shaved milk chocolate.

PUFFED RICE & CHOCOLATE BARK WITH MOUSSE & FRESH BERRIES

A dessert perfect for small get-togethers or for larger gatherings.

ABOUT 10 SERVINGS

Bark

About 4 oz dark chocolate
(65%)

1¾ oz puffed rice cereal

Mousse

4 oz dark chocolate (65–70%)

3 large eggs, separated

Garnish

9 oz fresh berries, such as
raspberries, blackberries,
and blueberries

Shaved dark chocolate

Chop the chocolate for the bark and melt it in a microwave or over a water bath. Remove from the heat and fold in the puffed rice. Spread the mixture as thin as possible on a piece of parchment paper. Let harden and break into pieces.

Coarsely chop the chocolate for the mousse and melt on low power in the microwave. Stir now and then. Lightly whisk the egg yolks and whisk the egg whites in another bowl until soft peaks form. Stir the egg yolks into the chocolate and then quickly fold in the egg whites.

Fill a disposable piping bag with the mousse and pipe dollops on the chocolate bark pieces. Garnish with fresh berries and shaved chocolate.

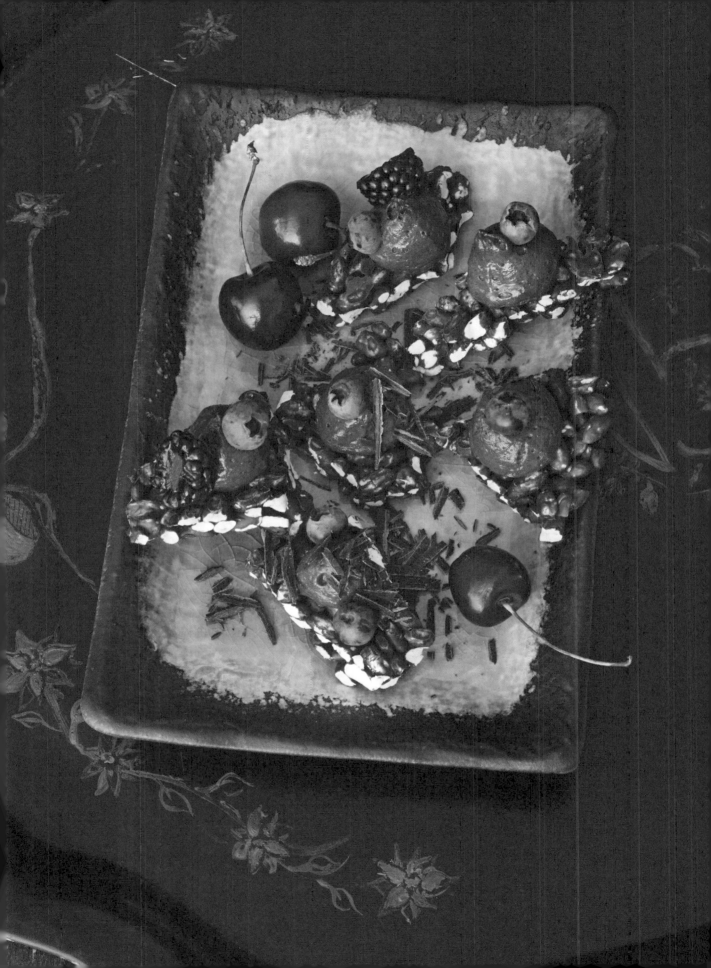

CHOCOLATE SAUCES

CHOCOLATE SAUCES

6-8 SERVINGS

Scant ½ cup cacao powder

¾ cup granulated sugar

1¼ cups water

DARK CHOCOLATE SAUCE 1-2-3

Combine the ingredients in a saucepan. Bring to a boil then simmer for about 7 minutes.

6-8 SERVINGS

5 oz milk chocolate

¾ cup heavy cream

1 tsp light corn syrup or glucose

1 tbsp room temperature butter

MILK CHOCOLATE SAUCE

Chop the chocolate and set aside. Bring the cream and syrup to a boil. Pour in the chocolate and stir in the butter until smooth.

6-8 SERVINGS

5 oz white chocolate

¼ cup water

⅔ cup heavy cream

2 tbsp granulated sugar

WHITE CHOCOLATE SAUCE

Coarsely chop the chocolate and place in a bowl. Boil the water, cream, and sugar for a few minutes and then pour over the chocolate. Stir until all the chocolate has melted.

FUDGE SAUCE

6–8 SERVINGS

⅔ cup heavy cream

75 g (about 5 tbsp) butter

½ cup packed light brown
sugar

2½ oz dark chocolate
(56–64%)

Bring the cream, butter, and brown sugar to a boil. Let it simmer for a few minutes and then remove from the heat. Chop the chocolate and place it in a bowl. Pour the sauce over the chocolate and stir until all the chocolate has melted.

SALTED FUDGE SAUCE

6–8 SERVINGS

1¾ oz light corn syrup

3 tbsp granulated sugar

3 tbsp heavy cream

50 g (about 3½ tbsp) butter

1 pinch salt

Boil the ingredients together for 5 minutes. Let cool to room temperature.

TRUFFLE CHOCOLATE SAUCE

6–8 SERVINGS

3½ oz dark chocolate
(54–68%)

¾ cup heavy cream

1 tbsp room temperature
butter

Coarsely chop the chocolate and place in a bowl. Bring the cream to a boil and pour it over the chocolate. Whisk until all the chocolate pieces have melted. Stir in the butter. Let cool.

DRINKS & CHOCOLATE

AZTEC CHOCOLATE

Xocoatl, or Kakauatl, is a magic aphrodisiac that was introduced by the Aztecs, who flavored the drink with different spices, honey or vanilla. A half cup of this aphrodisiac is enough—too much might make you drowsy. . .

4 CUPS

½ vanilla bean or 1 tsp vanilla sugar

4 tbsp cacao powder

4 tbsp granulated sugar

¾ cup heavy cream or milk

1 pinch ground cardamom seeds

1 cinnamon stick

1 star anise

3⅓ cups water

Split the vanilla bean and scrape out the seeds. Set aside. Combine the cacao powder, sugar, and cream or milk in a large heat-resistant pan. Bring the vanilla bean seeds, vanilla sugar, spices, and water to a boil and let simmer for a few minutes. Strain and pour the hot spiced water over the cacao mixture. Stir. Fill cups or glasses with the drink. Finish with a dollop of whipped cream and dust with cacao.

TIP!! Serve winter's most wonderful hot chocolate drink in tall, festive glasses. Spike with a few splashes of dark rum, or instead, let it boil with a bit of fresh chili or Spanish pepper. Top with whipped cream.

IRISH CHOCOLATE

A variation on Irish coffee with chocolate instead of coffee. Both whiskey and dark rum go well with this warm drink.

1 GLASS

2 tbsp heavy cream

1 tbsp light brown sugar

1 tbsp cacao powder

¾ cup milk

4½ tbsp Irish whiskey or
   dark rum

1 pinch ground coffee

Lightly whip the cream and set aside. Bring the brown sugar, cacao powder, and milk to a boil. Pour the whiskey or rum in a glass and pour in the chocolate mixture. Top with whipped cream and garnish with ground coffee.

WARM MINT CHOCOLATE

Perfect for a break on the ski slopes or cozy moments in a winter cabin.

1 CUP

2 tbsp heavy cream

1 tbsp raw sugar

1 tbsp cacao powder

¾ cup milk

4½ tbsp dark rum

1 disk of mint chocolate

1 pinch cacao powder
   or shaved chocolate

Lightly whip the cream and set aside. Bring the raw sugar, cacao powder, and milk to a boil. Pour the rum in a glass and then pour in the chocolate mixture. Add in the mint chocolate, top with whipped cream, and dust with cacao powder.

MILK CHOCOLATE SHAKE

Try this flavored with orange zest and decorated with berries.

1 GLASS

1 tsp chocolate sauce
   (see page 226)

¾ cup chocolate ice cream

⅔ cup milk

1 tsp shaved dark chocolate
   (64–85%)

Optional orange zest

Garnish

Fresh raspberries or
   blackberries

Pour the chocolate sauce in the bottom of a tall glass. Puree the rest of the ingredients, except for the chocolate, in a blender and pour into the glass. Garnish with shaved chocolate and optionally with the orange zest, and top with berries. Serve with a straw.

LICORICE & CHOCOLATE SHAKE

Licorice in a new way. You have to try this!

1 GLASS

1 tsp chocolate sauce
   (see page 226)

¾ cup chocolate ice cream

⅔ cup milk

1 tsp licorice powder

Garnish

Fresh raspberries

Pour the chocolate sauce in the bottom of a tall glass. Puree the rest of the ingredients in a blender and pour into the glass. Top with raspberries and serve.

SPICED CHOCOLATE

The flavor of this combination increases if you let it sit and steep for a few weeks. The chocolate absorbs the aroma of the spices. (This is called an infusion.)

1 BOWL OF CHOCOLATE, ABOUT 10 CUPS

5 oz dark chocolate (56–70%)

1¾ oz milk chocolate

1¾ oz white chocolate

¼ cup dried rose petals

1 tbsp fennel seeds

1 tbsp anise seeds

1 tbsp vanilla sugar

Chop the chocolate and combine with the spices. Store in a jar with an airtight lid. Bring a large cup of milk to a boil and then stir in a few spoonfuls of the spiced chocolate blend. Let steep for a few minutes and then strain.

TIP!! Dried rose petals can be bought at spice markets or well-stocked tea shops. If you want to dry your own rose petals from the garden, you can spread them on a rack and dry in a dry place at room temperature or on a tray in the sun for 1–2 days.

WHITE LAVENDER CHOCOLATE

Soft and smooth, this chocolate drink promotes a good night's sleep.

1 JAR OF CHOCOLATE, ABOUT 10 CUPS

7 oz white chocolate

3 tbsp lavender petals

1 tsp vanilla sugar

Chop the chocolate and combine with the lavender and vanilla sugar. Store in a jar with an airtight lid. Bring a large cup of milk to a boil and then stir in a few spoonfuls of the spiced chocolate blend. Let steep for a few minutes and then strain.

LIQUEURS

1 vanilla bean

7 oz cacao nibs

2 cups dark rum

½ cup raw sugar

CACAO LIQUEUR

Split the vanilla bean and place in a bottle with the cacao nibs. Pour in the rum and store in a cool place for 1–2 months. Strain and then whisk in the sugar.

½ cup crushed coffee beans

1½ cups cognac

½ cup raw sugar

1 tbsp muscovado sugar

COFFEE LIQUEUR

Place the beans in a bottle, pour in the cognac, and store in a cool place for 1–2 months. Strain and whisk in the raw sugar and muscovado sugar.

7 oz milk chocolate

1¼ cups heavy cream

¾ cup plus 2 tbsp Frangelico
  (hazelnut liqueur)

¾ cup dark rum

MILK CHOCOLATE LIQUEUR

Chop the chocolate and melt it together with the cream. Stir in the liqueur and rum. Pour into a bottle and keep cold. Serve on ice or drizzle over vanilla or chocolate ice cream as a dessert.

IMPORTANT!! This liqueur doesn't keep as long as the other liqueurs.

PAIRING DRINKS WITH CHOCOLATE

There's a lot to think about when it comes to pairing wine with chocolate. The chocolate's cacao content, bitterness, sweetness, and character strongly influence the taste experience.

RED WINE

Choosing the right wine with chocolate presents a fantastic taste experience. One ought to consider that the wine should be as sweet or sweeter than the chocolate or the dessert. Avoid wines with a lot of bitterness or acidity. The sweetness or bitterness in the chocolate only intensifies the acidity and bitterness in the wine, which makes the wine taste sour and the chocolate too sweet.

Preferred wines are sun-ripened and have a good, fruity sweetness, for example, a fruity Pinotage from South Africa or Amarone from Italy. The rule of thumb is the higher the cacao content, the more full-bodied the wine.

WHITE WINE

White wine is the preferred wine when pairing with white chocolate. Austrian and German dessert wines work well. Noble rot sweet sparkling wines from Asti, sweet champagne, and sparkling sake also go well with lighter milk chocolate desserts.

FORTIFIED WINE

When pairing dark chocolate with wine, fortified wines (*vins doux naturels*) are best. Which wine you choose depends on the dessert's components and character.

A lighter port wine of the ruby variety is a good match for a chocolate dessert with berries. If the dessert contains dried fruit and nuts, then a tawny port wine is better. Banyuls and Maury from South Africa is one such wine. Choose wines with a little burnt character such as Madeira or sweet sherry for crispy desserts with caramel and nuts. If the dessert is really powerful, with a high cacao content, and also very sweet, then it is best to use a PX sherry (from the dried grape Pedro Ximénez). Also, the wine Commandaria from Cyprus can support strong chocolate desserts. Other fortified wine varieties that go well are wines made with the muscat grape, such as the wine Muscadel from South Africa and Moscatel de Setúbal from Portugal. In Argentina there are also sweet strong wines made with the Malbec grape.

Because white chocolate doesn't contain the cacao mass, only cacao butter, the chocolate isn't as bitter as dark chocolate. It is powerfully sweet and requires a really sweet wine. Preferably a sweet noble rot wine of the Sauternes variety.

LIQUEURS AND FRUIT WINES

Different types of liqueurs also pair well with chocolate desserts. The flavor of the liqueur determines which chocolate dessert one chooses. Fruit wines such as cherry wine go well with dark chocolate desserts.

BEER

Beer and chocolate are also a good combination. A dark beer with sweetness and a roasted character, for example, a stout, cloister beer, or a porter, goes well with moist and sweet mud cake, brownies, and chocolate cake. The sweet chocolate brings out the heartiness and bitterness in the beer. Wheat beer and milk chocolate complement each other well.

LIQUOR AND HARD ALCOHOL

Pure spirits generally do not contain a sweetness that matches the sweetness in chocolate, but you can try to find other complementary flavor profiles to pair.

Distilled drinks that have been barrel-aged for some time usually come closer to flavor profiles in common with chocolate. In a barrel-aged cognac or Armagnac, you can find tones of vanilla and caramel, and in barrel-aged rum from the West Indies, toffee tones of muscovado sugar and coffee. Other similar distilled liquors include calvados and brandy. Aged tequila is a real "wild card" well worth trying.

CERTIFIED CHOCOLATE

BIODYNAMIC

Biodynamic farming is a form of organic agriculture based in anthroposophy. Biodynamic farming follows planetary cycles and supports the earth's ecological systems. Composting plays a key role in biodynamic agriculture, as does recycling and observing the movement of the constellations. Biodynamic farming can be certified by the Demeter Association label.

ORGANIC

There is high demand for organic chocolate. Today, the majority of large chocolate manufacturers make organic chocolate, but there are many producers who specialize solely in cultivating, manufacturing, and selling organic chocolate. Growing ecologically means that the chocolate comes from cacao growers who do not use chemical pesticides, GMOs (genetically modified organisms), or fertilizers. There are a number of different certifications for organic chocolate.

FAIR TRADE

Fair Trade means fair dealing and trading. Many small chocolate and food producers in developing countries are forced to sell their products for unreasonably low prices via middlemen who take large cuts of the earnings. This creates unbearable working conditions and, in some cases, means child labor. Fair Trade is a response to this. Fair Trade is not assistance but a trading partnership between producers, importers, stores, and consumers that is based on the idea that the producers should receive fair payment and have good working conditions, as well as have their human rights respected and have the opportunity to farm organically. This enables both short- and long-term economic and social development. There are four major international organizations that work with fair trading practices: FLO, WFTO, NEWS!, and EFTA. Many cacao producers are still critical of Fair Trade and other certifications because they think it costs too much and that the money ends up in the wrong hands. The cacao farmers have therefore started their own cooperative in order to improve their conditions.

KOSHER-CERTIFIED ORGANIC CHOCOLATE

Equal Exchange in Switzerland produces a kosher-certified organic chocolate.

PREMIUM, GRAND CRU & DELUXE

These labels, which are used for marketing, have nothing to do with quality certification. Instead, look for chocolate with natural ingredients.

RAINFOREST ALLIANCE CERTIFIED

Rainforest Alliance means that it is rainforest-certified. This is a seal that shows respect for the environment and humanity. The Rainforest Alliance organization works with agriculture, forestry, and tourism to preserve and spread knowledge about our environment, both animal and plant life, for the future. For those who support themselves through tourism, it is important to respect the rainforest environment in which they live. The companies who live up to this philosophy receive certification, as well as those companies that process ready-made products with raw ingredients. Consumption has a great impact on how we manage our natural resources, and consuming certified products contributes to better conditions for the environment, humans, and animals in these sensitive regions.

RAW CHOCOLATE

Raw chocolate contains more antioxidants than ordinary chocolate, which makes it more nutritious. Chocolate that is produced according to the raw food principle (raw chocolate) is not heated more than 108°F in order not to destroy the antioxidants. These exact numbers are naturally difficult to maintain, and many raw chocolate producers fall somewhere between 113 and 120°F.

SINGLE

Single designations are intended to help consumers determine the nuances of chocolate flavors. It is a direction on a flavor map that is often necessary because cacao beans are influenced by geography, climate, soil quality, and bean variety. This way, one can discover, for example, the fruity and slightly acidic character of the trinitario bean from Madagascar, the soft, flowery Cacao Nacional from Ecuador, and the tough, rustic, and smoky trinitario from Trinidad.

SINGLE ESTATE OR CRU DE PLANTATION

If the chocolate is marked with some of these labels, it means that the cacao beans come from the same plantation.

SINGLE ORIGIN OR CRU D'ORIGINE

This label means that the chocolate is made with cacao all from the same country or region.

THE HISTORY OF CHOCOLATE

4000 B.C.
The cacao tree has its origins in the shaded valleys around the Amazon River where it is said to have grown since 4000 B.C.

600 A.D.
The Mayan people in Central America begin growing the cacao tree.

1000 A.D.
The cacao bean has become a valuable trading good.

800–1100 A.D.
According to Aztec mythology, it was the god Quetzalcóatl who brought cacao to the earth. People learned to worship the tree that they called Cachuaquahitl, which was supposed to be a source of power and wealth. From these fruits, the gods prepared a drink: *Theobroma cacao*, "food of the gods cacao." Quetzalcóatl was banished from this paradise, but the humans never stopped waiting for him. In the 1500s, they probably confused Hernán Cortés with this Aztec god, which made it easier for Cortés to control the cacao.

1200S
The Aztecs conquer the Mayan people and cacao is said to have been some of the plunder of war.

1502
Christopher Columbus lands on the island of Guanaja off the coast of Honduras and the natives invite him to the welcome drink Cacauarl—cacao water. This is made from cacao paste blended with spices and cornmeal and then shaken in a clay pot. Columbus takes the cacao bean back to the Spanish court, which reacts coolly toward both the drink and the cacao beans.

1519
The Spanish conqueror Hernán Cortés lands in Mexico. He also gets to try a chocolate drink called Xocoatl that is served in a golden goblet and has great religious significance.

1524
Hernán Cortés sends home cacao beans to the Spanish court. About the same time, sugar from the East Indies and vanilla from Mexico are introduced, preparing the way for the cacao bean.

1530-40

Spanish nuns in Guanaco discover that one can improve the taste of the cacao drink by adding sugar and vanilla.

1569

Pope Pius V confirms that the cacao drink does not break fasting, which quickly makes it popular.

1606

Explorer Francesco Carletti returns to Florence from his voyages in the "Oriental Indies" and introduces chocolate to Italy.

1631

The first scientific work on chocolate, written by Dr. Colmenero de Ledesma, debuts.

1659

Englishmen establish the first cacao plantation in Jamaica. At the same time, David Chaillou opens the first chocolate shop in Paris on the Rue de l'Arbre-Sec.

1680

The word "chocolat" shows up for the first time in a French dictionary.

1690

Chocolate makes its debut in Sweden. In an encyclopedia from the time, there is a recipe with the name "Sioccolade."

1705

The first critical voices make themselves heard when Frenchman Daniel Duncan expresses his concern regarding the misuse of tea, coffee, and chocolate.

1755

North America discovers chocolate. Meanwhile in Sweden, Cajsa Warg's classic cookbook comes out, and it contains recipes for several chocolate dishes.

1756

France begins mechanized production of chocolate.

1760

The first French chocolate factory, Chocolatier Royal, opens in Paris. The factory uses cacao beans from the French colonies.

1819

The first Swiss chocolate factory is opened.

1822

The first cacao tree in Africa is planted.

1828

A completely new technique is tested in Holland using chemist Coenraad van Houten's cacao press, which separates the cacao butter from the cacao powder and makes a smooth and fine chocolate.

1868

Theodor Tobler begins making chocolate in Switzerland: the nougat, almond, and honey chocolate called Toblerone, whose tops are inspired by the Matterhorn mountain.

1875

The first milk chocolate is produced by Daniel Peter in Switzerland. He uses German chemist Henri Nestlé's discovery of condensed milk, which is processed to powdered milk, and adds this to the chocolate.

1872–78

Cloetta Chocolate Factory is founded in Malmö, Sweden by the brothers Cloetta from Switzerland.

1879

Rodolphe Lindt introduces a new type of smooth chocolate that is rolled back and forth. This method is called conching and lays the groundwork for the chocolate we eat today.

1883

The first boutique in the world-famous chain Côte d'Or opens in Belgium.

1888

The Mazetti chocolate factory opens its doors in Malmö. The founder is a Dane, Emile Nissen. The factory is called Malmö Chocolate & Confection Factory until 1947 when its name was changed to Mazetti. Today, the premises hold a museum and the Malmö Chocolate Factory.

1891

In Finland, the Swiss chocolate maker Karl Fazer starts his company, Fazer, that later is merged with Cloetta (only to separate again a little later on).

1895

Freia Chocolate Factory is opened in Oslo. It is the same company that in 1916 opens Marabou Stockholm.

1911

The Belgian family Callebaut begins making chocolate bars.

1912

Belgian Jean Neuhaus begins producing chocolate bars with wrapping paper decorated with a picture of an elephant, and he also begins production of his well-known Belgian pralines. Belgian pralines are often bigger than French ones, and they often contain milk chocolate and nuts.

1923

The first chocolate bar is launched in the American market by Frank Mars.

1995

Quality chocolate begins to appear in Sweden, chocolate that is made in France, Belgium, and Spain. People begin talking about different types of cacao beans and tempering techniques.

2005-10

Organic chocolate starts showing up in shops, albeit on a small scale, and the Swedes are quick to respond to the organically grown chocolate. In France, the focus is on Fair Trade, which might have something to do with the country's relationship to its former colonies. Raw chocolate widens throughout the market, a result of the healthy raw food culture started a few years earlier in California. People also begin working with wild cacao from Bolivia. Suddenly there is interest in small-scale production of the highest quality chocolate.

TODAY

There are a number of chocolate makers who produce chocolate bars sold all over the world. New, large markets include Japan, China, and the Middle East, where earlier there was no tradition of either eating or making chocolate. Trendy new chocolate bars have opened in different places around world in places such as Zurich, Geneva, Paris, and Tokyo, among others.

GLOSSARY

BAR Healthy, sweet bites are usually called bars, but chocolate can also take the form of a "bar," so the word "bar" can mean either one.

CERTIFICATION In order to find more information about chocolate bars than is available on the packaging, you can use their certification (see pages 240–241).

CUPS Open chocolate molds.

DULCE DE LECHE Caramelized sweetened condensed milk. It is cooked to a soft caramel cream common in South American ice cream and desserts.

FONDANT Popular warm chocolate pastry that soon is available in as many different varieties as apple pie and probably is one of the recipes that has traveled most around the world. Renowned French chef Michel Bras stands by the first recipe.

GANACHE Chocolate filling or icing that is basically made from boiled cream and chocolate. One usually sweetens the ganache with honey or corn syrup. For a shiny and delicate ganache, you can mix in a little butter.

GRANULATED LICORICE Licorice powder made from pure licorice root that is boiled and dried and gives a concentrated, natural licorice flavor. Check out baking supply companies online to find out more information about granulated licorice and licorice powder.

MOLDING Tempered chocolate is molded in forms. Tempering allows the chocolate to solidify, becoming hard and shiny, but also ensures that it contracts and shrinks, which helps it release from the molds.

NIBS Shelled, dried, or roasted and crushed cacao beans (also called grué).

PISTOLE Small chocolate disks with different flavors and spices; they are one of the earliest known French-manufactured chocolate confections.

PRALINE A chocolate bite that can be molded or cut into pieces and dipped in chocolate. French pralines usually are small and weigh $1/3$–$1/2$ oz. Belgian pralines are usually bigger and weigh at least $1/2$ oz. They are often a little sweeter and made with milk chocolate and nut fillings.

PRALINÉ Hazelnut filling that is made from roasted, caramelized hazelnuts mixed until they become oily and creamy. Adding melted chocolate creates a filling called Gianduja. Adding caramelized almonds to the first phase of the nut blending keeps the mixture crumbly (before it becomes oily), and thus it becomes a croquant. The word comes from the French word "croquant" that means crunchy.

RAW CHOCOLATE Chocolate that is produced organically and with extra care. It should not be heated above 108°F in order to preserve as much nutrition and fine taste as possible.

SEALING PRALINES Sealing the bottom of the praline by spreading tempered chocolate over the bottom and scraping away the excess chocolate with a scraper.

TEMPERING Process that makes the chocolate hard and shiny.

TERRINE An oval or rectangular mold. The word comes from the French "terrine" which has its origin in the Latin word "terra," or "clay," because these forms were earlier made from clay.

TRUFFLE A truffle can be made in the same way as ganache. There are an infinite number of different recipes and flavors: among others, whipped truffles, cream truffles, and butter truffles. The name "truffle" refers to the shape. One rolls a ball that is then rolled in cacao and thus looks like the truffle mushroom from which it derives its name. Ganache and truffle are fairly similar. It is the rolled variety that makes it a truffle. However, many call ganache a truffle, truffle icing, or truffle filling because they are made with the same ingredients. But that actually isn't correct.

INDEX

THANKS

SANTIAGO AND CARLA PERALTA at Pacari, who guided us in Quito, Ecuador, and in their factory, and who shared a fantastic eight-course chocolate menu.

KERSTI LILJEQVIST ZEBEDA at Zebeda Chocolate AB, agent for Pacari, who helped procure all the fine ingredients.

WILSON AND JUAN LEÓN MERA at Kallari, who guided us to the indigenous village where we got to roast our own cacao.

EQ TOURING / EXCLUSIVE GALAPAGOS, New York, **ISABELL JARAMILLO**, our guide **WILLY** and our driver **JORGE**.

KERSTIN BERGFORS, publisher at Bonnier Fakta, who gave me the opportunity to make this book.

STEFAN WETTAINEN, photographer, for incredibly beautiful and cool photos.

SUSANNA BLÅVARG, photographer on the trip to Ecuador, for your amazing pictures, right on target and attractive as always! Thanks also for all the resources and everything you did for the trip!

VIGGO BLÅVARG, for good company on the trip and for your brilliant recipe tips.

ELISABETH BJÖRKBOM, designer, for your accurate, contemporary design and for your positive and inspiring attitude toward chocolate!

ANN PÅLSSON at Ann Pålsson Media & Kommunication AB, for editorial help.

ANNIKA STRÖM AND LINNEA VON ZWEIGBERGK, editors at Bonnier Fakta.

CONNY JOHANSSON, my husband, for following me to Ecuador, and for your help with the wine and drinks text.

KERSTIN GRÄBNER, my mother, for all your support and administrative help.

RASMUS BO BOJESEN AND PETER HANSSON at the Malmö Chocolate Factory, for the wild cacao beans you gave me and for the chance to taste your Oialla chocolate.

KRISTINA VALENTIN, for your help.

PER MATTSSON, pastry chef and chocolatier, who treated me to his fantastic pralines made from organic chocolate from Venezuela, which sparked my interest in organic chocolate.

JAN DANIELSSON, pastry chef and chocolatier, for the time I got to work with you at Källhagens Värdshus. It was both inspiring and instructive!

JAN HEDH, for all the inspiration and knowledge you have shared with me.

MAGNUS JOHANSSON AND TONY OLSSON, for gilding every year with the Stockholm Chocolate Festival.